The *Pastoral Vision* of Cormac McCarthy

NUMBER EIGHTEEN:
Tarleton State University
Southwestern Studies in the Humanities
William T. Pilkington
General Editor

THE *Pastoral Vision* OF Cormac McCarthy

GEORG GUILLEMIN

TEXAS A&M
UNIVERSITY PRESS
College Station

FIRST EDITION

The paper used in this book meets the minimum requirements
of the American National Standard for Permanence
of Paper for Printed Library Materials, Z39.48–1984.
Binding materials have been chosen for durability.
∞

Frontispiece: Cormac McCarthy,
courtesy MAGNUMPHOTOS

Library of Congress Cataloging-in-Publication Data
Guillemin, Georg.
The pastoral vision of Cormac McCarthy / Georg Guillemin.—1st ed.
p. cm. — (Tarleton State University southwestern studies in the humanities ; no. 18)
Includes bibliographical references and index.
ISBN 1-58544-341-7 (alk. paper)
1. McCarthy, Cormac, 1933—Criticism and interpretation. 2. Pastoral fiction, American—History and criticism. 3. Mexican-American Border Region—In literature. 4. Southern States—In literature. 5. Tennessee, East—In literature. 6. Country life in literature. I. Title. II. Series.
PS3563.C337Z67 2004
813'.54—dc22
2203023763

For Dianne, Chip, and Rick

For that which befalleth the sons of man befalleth beasts;
even one thing befalleth them:
as the one dieth, so dieth the other;
yea, they have all one breath;
so that a man hath no preeminence above a beast:
for all is vanity.

ECCLESIASTES 3:19

Contents

The *Pastoral Vision* of Cormac McCarthy

Introduction

The Prototypical *Suttree*

> The more we learn about nature, the more its reiterative meaninglessness will appall us. Ultimate horror lies not in the heart of darkness but in the heart of enlightened understanding of nature.
>
> Karl Kroeber, *Ecological Literary Criticism*

The most intriguing literary aspect of McCarthy's fiction is that his narrative voice is increasingly at odds with his narrative vision. McCarthy pitches a highly stylized, wholly man-made literary practice against his evolving ecopastoral universe, until a stalemate between humanist discourse and posthumanist idea invests his fiction with a narrative melancholia that is actually very common in pastoral fiction. Out of the dialectic tension between narrative voice and narrative vision, however, evolves a version of pastoral without equal in the American literature of the latter half of the twentieth century. The subject of this comprehensive study will be the evolution of McCarthy's work: the shift from traditional pastoralism in *The Orchard Keeper* (1965) to the wilderness turn in *Child of God* (1973), and from the anti-pastoralism of *Outer Dark* (1968) to the negative biocentrism of *Blood Meridian* (1985) and finally to the ecopastoralism of the Border Trilogy.[1]

The study is based on the assumption that a compositional triangle is at play throughout McCarthy's work. One side of the triangle is formed by a pervasive spirit of melancholia, used—in keeping with a tradition going back to baroque times (or even biblical times)—as a literary device for creating narrative distance. In a way, melancholia itself seems to narrate the novels. Another side of the triangle is allegoresis, the encryption of narrative contents in parabolic images and story lines in the manner of fables. On the third side of the triangle we find the pastoral theme, understood as the principal quest for harmony in a better world. All the novels mentioned above are defined by the interaction of melancholy mood, allegorical style, and pastoral theme.

The one novel not mentioned, *Suttree* (1979), does not invite inclusion into a pastoral review of McCarthy's work. It stands out because of its urban setting, and therefore contains few nature scenes that would validate a pastoral reading. It may, however, be used as the perfect introduction to McCarthy's style, being, as it were, McCarthy's longest novel and the most complex. *Suttree* marks a halfway point in McCarthy's fiction, not just because it was the fourth novel published but also because it concludes the cycle of Southern novels. In some respects *Suttree* might count as his most Southern work (due to the tall tales, banter, and local color), while in other respects it seems barely American (due to its use of stream of consciousness and its Old World iconography).

Actually, *Suttree* is less a pivotal than a prototypical work. McCarthy began to work on the novel in the early 1960s (before he wrote *The Orchard Keeper*), and it reads like a debut novel: Dense description alternates with the lean prose of the plot action; loquacious monologues with idiomatic dialogue; isolated episodes with a vaguely linear story line; autobiographical hints with intertextual links. Then again, the book draws on the writing experience of the three foregoing novels. Like these it uses expository tableaux, scenes of violence, and episodic tangents to describe the protagonist's psyche.

In the context of discussing McCarthy's pastoralism, the singularity of *Suttree* constitutes not so much a challenge as a windfall. As a prototypical work, the novel contains all the compositional elements that will be essential for the individual interpretations of the novels. A selective discussion of these elements will introduce the intended critical approach without preempting the discussion of the larger context. This critical sleight of hand—involving *Suttree* in precisely the kind of reading it does not accommodate—will serve to define three compositional mainstays in McCarthy's writings: the above-mentioned elements of pastoral genre, allegorical style, and melancholy perspective. In each of McCarthy's novels these elements interact to form a tripartite structure that showcases the author's aesthetic order. The combination makes sense, for melancholy subject matter generally favors allegorical parables either of self-deprecation or self-empowerment, while pastoral narratives generally favor utopian parables of escape into a better, simpler world. And as he acknowledges the futility of his escapism, the pastoral narrator tends to succumb to melancholia.

Suttree is set in the Knoxville of the early 1950s, or, more precisely, in the urban wasteland of McAnally Flats, a depressed neighborhood adjacent to the Tennessee River and part of downtown Knoxville. The novel's wealth of authentic detail reflects the fact that McCarthy grew up and went to college in that town.[2] The text introduces the district as "a world within the world" (4), a microcosm of speakeasies, black shantytowns, and houseboats (one of which the protagonist Cornelius Suttree inhabits). The stark representation of this "terra damnata" (306) from Suttree's point of view recalls the literary tradition of the gentleman observer mingling with the poorest of the poor.

Coming from a bourgeois family background, this "reprobate scion of doomed Saxon clans" (136) has renounced his Catholic faith, social status, and career prospects to become a fisherman. Among Suttree's pariah friends is young Gene Harrogate, one of McCarthy's likable but never-do-well picaro figures. At their first encounter in the workhouse, Harrogate is incarcerated for sexually abusing watermelons. All his schemes reveal similar maturity and resourcefulness, such as his plan to dynamite his way into a bank vault that results in his breaching a sewer main instead. Along with the idiomatic banter, roughhousing, and tall tales, the humor of this picaresque story line constitutes a counter-discourse to the existential gloom of the novel's bulk. After two abortive romances, a pilgrimage into the Appalachians, and the discovery of a dead man in his own bed (suggesting he had survived his own death) Suttree eventually leaves the city and takes to the road. The novel ends with an image reminiscent of Dante's "The Wood of the Suicides," in which black hounds terrorize the souls.[3] The narrator addresses the reader directly in seeming abdication of both urban civilization and agrarian pastoralism:

> An enormous lank hound had come out of the meadow by the river like a hound from the depths and was sniffing at the spot where Suttree had stood.
>
> Somewhere in the gray wood by the river is the huntsman and in the brooming corn and in the castellated press of the cities. His work lies all wheres and his hounds tire not. (471)

This conclusion connects directly to a passage in the prologue in which, analogously, death is said to besiege the city; the references here are again to Dante, to Poe's "The Masque of the Red Death," and to Melville's weaver god in *Moby Dick* (446): "The city beset by a thing unknown and will it come from forest or sea? The murengers have walled the pale, the gates are shut, but lo the thing's inside and can you guess his shape? Where he's kept and what's the counter of his face? Is he a weaver, bloody shuttle shot through a timewarp, a carder of souls from the world's nap? Or a hunter with hounds or do bone horses draw his deadcart through the streets and does he call his trade to each?" (*Suttree* 4–5) The liberal use of intertextuality here suggests not so much a postmodern pastiche with indeterminate meaning but rather, creates a passage that reads like the back-reference typical of allegorical writing, the implied threat being death.

In short, *Suttree* combines a picaresque quest for survival with a modernist quest for truth, a baroque style with existentialist despair. The novel sustains comparisons to Eliot's "Waste Land" and Camus's *Myth of Sisyphus* (1942), to Joyce's *Ulysses* (1918) and Selby's *Last Exit to Brooklyn* (1957), and to Twain's *Huckleberry Finn* and Dante's *The Divine Comedy*.[4] It invites a close reading of its iconography as much as it invites psychoanalysis. But in spite of its complexity, the novel manifests a unified composition.

In discussing McCarthy's aesthetic, it is essential to note that the melancholia underlying the narrative process does not originate in pastoral nostalgia. On the contrary, the pastoral theme of loss seems chosen as a suitable articulation of melancholia as such. Melancholia appears in McCarthy's writings in the form of an obsession with death or mortality, as well as in a consistent maintenance of narrative distance. Such melancholy distancing, understood as a time-honored literary device, originates in the biblical image of the agonized prophet on the hill who watches the world from afar on its course toward ruin. In the novel at hand, this conceit is used, for instance, when Suttree associates the rubble of a riverside lot with the emblem used by the Puritans to invoke the divine sanction of their mission: "[A]ll this detritus slid from the city on the hill" (411). Here, the narrative melancholia is translated into the protagonist's despondency as well as into his inability or unwillingness to assume any form of civic responsibility.

Suttree's self-chosen outcast status is never fully explained beyond a deep-seated resentment of the bourgeois pattern of domesticity, prosperity, and morality. He has abandoned his wife but continues to be traumatized by losing first her and later his child, "choked with a sorrow he had never known" (153). Yet his primitive life revolves around nothing at all, and its meaninglessness horrifies him just as much. In a scene reminiscent of mad King Lear on the heath, his quest for meaning takes a suicidal turn: "Suttree stood among the screaming leaves and called the lightning down. It cracked and boomed about and he pointed out the darkened heart within him and cried for light. If there be any art in the weathers of this earth. Or char these bones to coal. If you can, if you can. A blackened rag in the rain" (366).

In the sense that plot and exposition are organized around the search for the meaning of life and death, *Suttree* parallels the part of Quentin Compson in Faulkner's *The Sound and the Fury* (1929). Both characters have an academic background; both are haunted by their families' past. Here, as there, suicidal neuroses articulate themselves in obsessions with time and the chiaroscuro of light.[5] Among the relevant passages counts a childhood memory of a horse race in which Suttree's grandfather offers

> that simple comparison of rotary motions and in the oratory to which he was prone that they had witnessed a thing against which time would not prevail.
>
> He meant a thing to be remembered, but the young apostate by the rail at his elbow had already begun to sicken at the slow seeping of life. He could see the shape of the skull through the old man's flesh. Hear sand in the glass. Lives running out like something foul, nightsoil from a cesspipe, a measured dripping in the dark. The clock has run, the horse has run, and which has measured which? (136)

On a personal level, then, the novel reads like a psychological profile of its main character. From among the sermons of evangelists Suttree picks the jeremiads, a family photo album resembles a "picturebook of the afflicted" (130), a snake under a rock is hailed as "little brother death" (284), and his hard-drinking uncle has a "smell of death at the edges" (16). Suttree's sensory spectrum is fine-tuned to aspects of mortality. He provokes life-threatening experiences as if to seek death, involving himself in brawls, contracting typhoid, sustaining severe injury, and starving himself during his hike into the Gatlinburg wilderness. With the reclusive ragpicker he converses about God and dying. The ragman admits, "I always figured they was a God" but "I just never did like him" (147), and Suttree feels the same way. His skepticism and a longing for death inform his idea that "Death is what the living carry with them. A state of dread, like some uncanny foretaste of a bitter memory. But the dead do not remember and nothingness is not a curse. Far from it" (153).

Upon closer scrutiny, the melancholia apparent in Suttree and in the narrator of *Suttree* loses some of its mournful aspect and is in fact drained of any emotion whatsoever. Its intrinsic nature is the catatonic state described in William James's lecture on the "sick soul."[6] What James says about Tolstoy could be applied to Suttree, namely that the perceived meaninglessness of life "was like those first discomforts of a sick man, to which he pays but little attention till they run into one continuous suffering, and then he realizes that what he took for a passing disorder means the most momentous thing in the world for him, means his death" (153). James suggests that sentiments of such emotionally deadened melancholia do not originate in the subject's physical or social reality, but "have their source in another sphere of existence altogether, in the animal and spiritual region of the subject's being. Conceive yourself, if possible, suddenly stripped of all the emotion with which your world now inspires you, and try to imagine it *as it exists,* purely by itself, without your favorable or unfavorable, hopeful or apprehensive comment. It will be almost impossible for you to realize such a condition of negativity and deadness" (150). The state of mind James describes essentially captures not only the meaninglessness that perturbs Suttree, but, moreover, the narrative perspective governing McCarthy's writings in general. It is precisely this melancholy equanimity that conditions the pastoral vision of McCarthy. If optimistically interpreted, its pessimistic indifference bestows an egalitarian existential status on all terrestrial phenomena alike. James's words support this line of argument as he arrives at the following conclusion: "No one portion of the universe would then have importance beyond another; and the whole collection of its things and series of its events would be without significance, character, expression, or perspective" (150).

What is most important, then, about the death-centeredness of *Suttree* is that death assumes a leveling function. The narrative form transporting the egalitarian aspect of death in effect simulates the folkloric emblem of Death personified, which comes for each and every person regardless of status. Relevant images include dreams of the dead: "In a dream I walked with my grandfather by a dark lake and the old man's talk was filled with incertitude. I saw how all things false fall from the dead. We spoke easily and I was humbly honored to walk with him deep in that world where he was a man like all men" (14). Toward the end of *Suttree,* after "[t]he wilderness has treated him with a sublime indifference" (Longley 87) and after the typhoid fever has failed to carry him off, melancholia gives way to the affirmative insight "I know all souls are one and all souls lonely" (459). Elsewhere, this notion is rephrased in a way that calls to mind transcendentalist writing or Whitman's[7] poetry: "It is not alone in the dark of death that all souls are one soul" (414). In the course of the same soliloquy, Suttree comes to renounce his modernist quest for a stable sense of self, though no post-humanist implication reveals itself yet: "I spoke with bitterness about my life and I said that I would take my own part against the slander of oblivion and against the monstrous facelessness of it and that I would stand a stone in the very void where all would read my name. Of that vanity I recant all" (414).[8] On the plot level of the text, this moment of epiphany provides the novel's theme of suicide with "a resolution to the very problem central to 'The Myth of Sisyphus,' and one presented with elements strikingly in common with that work. While many readers of *Suttree* have felt that the novel simply stops, it does resolve itself and does so in the same way as Camus's work: in an act of will rather than an act of rational thought" (Shelton 72).

On the meta-narrative level, however, the cause and resolution of Suttree's crisis matter less than the fact that his fixation on death creates a protagonist with a melancholy point of view. Among McCarthy's novels, *Suttree* is the only one with an intellectually active protagonist, while in all his novels the narrative perspective coincides with the protagonists' points of view. In a prototypical manner, *Suttree* shows how the protagonist's melancholia is indistinguishable from that of the narrative consciousness. In other words, although character and narrator are distinct entities, they virtually share a point of view. Since he channels the narrative perspective, Suttree's focus on death creates the cognitive condition for subjecting all that is seen and all that is told to the death-centered vision of the melancholy narrator. Analogously, the protagonists of all the other novels function as vessels for the narrative gaze even as the narrators remain amorphous, and even if most of McCarthy's figures come across as curiously lifeless. In book after book, these unreflective nomads represent a melancholia that they do not contain within themselves.

The uneasy reception with which McCarthy's writings have occasionally been met may be due not so much to the author's penchant for violent action, but to his rhetoric and iconography. McCarthy is a storyteller in a parabolic sense. The secret of his symbolism is that it works not symbolically but allegorically at a time when allegoresis has just begun to regain respect as a literary mode. Its semantic single-mindedness renders allegory alien to the romantic, realist, or modernist schools of literature. Some postmodern writing has rehabilitated allegoresis through its use of parable, and typological structure through its use of intertextuality. But McCarthy can hardly be considered a postmodern writer. Any de-centering intention he may share with postmodernism owes less to the influence of fashionable theory than to the subversive energy of the grotesque. His allegorical iconography partakes of the realism Mikhail Bakhtin has defined as carnivalesque. A case in point, Suttree's hallucination during his wilderness quest calls to mind Shakespeare's *Midsummer Night's Dream,* Goethe's *Faust II,* or the tableaux of Hieronymous Bosch. The use of the grotesque is as typical of McCarthy's style as the mannerism of the run-on sentences: "And along the little ways in the rain and lightning came a troupe of squalid merrymakers bearing a caged wivern on shoulderpoles and other alchemical game, chimeras and cacodemons skewered up on boarspears and a pharmacopoeia of hellish condiments adorning a trestle and toted by trolls with an eldern gnome for guidon who shouted foul oaths from his mouthhole and a piper who piped a pipe of cloverbone and wore on his hip a glass flasket of some foul smoking fuel that yawed within viscid as quicksilver" (287–88). The problem of allegorical discourse is that it retards its own interpretation. It fails to signify anything beyond the finite meaning it confers through parable or type. The following emblem easily translates into the Ophelia motif, but what to make of it? "In an old grandfather time a ballad transpired here, some love gone wrong and a sabletressed girl drowned in an icegreen pool where she was found with her hair spreading like ink on the cold and cobbled river floor" (283). No context is given; the image presents itself without preparation and comment and is dropped again. Emblems like this one abound in *Suttree* and in McCarthy's novels generally. The insertion of these emblems must seem arbitrary if the text is approached with realistic criteria, and critics who have so approached it tend to write themselves into a rage.[9]

Actually, McCarthy's craftsmanship does not suggest that anything is left to chance or escapes narrative control even if his novels are not laid out to foreground plot progression, denouement, or character development. The plots progress, and the characters develop, to the degree that they serve to accumulate, rather than order, installments of a certain story as if to complete a mosaic of stills rather than to scroll a film in linear sequence. McCarthy's texts may therefore repeat intratextual stories or emblems and connect to stories told elsewhere by McCarthy or by other writers. They often affect a retold quality that is indigenous to oral storytelling and overrides the concerns of dramatic structure and mimetic exposition. In order not to end in a diagnosis of structural paucity, critical studies of McCarthy would do well to focus on the allegorical composition that gathers the emblems, banter, tall tales, and monotonous syntax into a unified aesthetic.

The effects of allegoresis in *Suttree* are impossible to overlook. The novel's prologue is all parable, explicitly establishing the textual setting as a stage. The baroque idea that the world represents a stage fronting for a higher form of being, and, inversely, that text and stage represent the world in microcosm, is the very presupposition of McCarthy's aesthetic.

> The rest indeed is silence. It has begun to rain. Light summer rain, you can see it falling slant in the town lights. The river lies in a grail of quietude. Here from the bridge the world below seems a gift of simplicity. Curious, no more.
>
> [. . .] A curtain is rising on the western world. A fine rain of soot, dead beetles, anonymous small bones. The audience sits webbed in dust. Within the gutted sockets of the interlocutor's skull a spider sleeps and the jointed ruins of the hanged fool dangle from the flies, bone pendulum in motley. Fourfooted shapes go to and fro over the boards. Ruder forms survive. (5)

Apart from its allegorical quality, the excerpt contains emblematic allusions to melancholia (the skull, the dust-covered audience, the watcher on the bridge) and the hope of survival. The narrative tension between the prologue's descriptions of urban squalor and the concluding emblem does not seem intended to qualify a Dickensian scenery with a sense of irony. Rather, it places in typological sequence two images of the world, one describing it as a pest house and the other describing it as a stage. The latter represents the very image underlying the passage from *Macbeth* from which Faulkner also took his title *The Sound and the Fury*.[10] What is added to the familiar image is that the theater seems decommissioned, bypassed by time, while "ruder forms" than audience, actors, and interlocutor—that is, creatures less refined—"survive." The survivalist notion, while originating in the retrospective melancholia of the text, implies a narrative indifference toward these cultural artifacts. At the same time, it invests life forms with existential privileges that do not share in the high drama of life. Thus, a sense of rivalry between a tragic view of life and a comic one surfaces, and this aspect ushers in the essence of McCarthy's pastoral vision.

What few pastoral aspects are found in *Suttree* manage to run the whole gamut of American pastoralism. For one thing, *Suttree* describes a ruined mansion, "which might have been lifted from the pages of any southern pastoral lament," while the novel remains free of pastoral nostalgia. The reader will look "in vain for the great theme of 'the past in the present,' for the burden of southern history, for . . . the conflict between tradition and modernity" (Grammer 30). A daydream occurring as Suttree walks the crumbling halls of the mansion and "through the ruined garden" contains the words "[s]omething more than time has passed here" (136). The scene obviously refers to Southern pastoralism in the emblem of the ruined mansion and ruined garden as something so anachronistic that it has ceased to be an object even of nostalgia. In this sense the scene reduces literary back-references, such as to Sutpen's mansion in Faulkner's *Absalom, Absalom!* (1936), to the function of stage props and discourages any elegiac or tragic reading of the novel. To read it in an anti-pastoral sense would equally miss the point, because pastoral escapism as a lifestyle choice is clearly still available to Suttree, as his wilderness trip demonstrates. The mansion, then, functions like a prop representing an anachronistic pastoral nostalgia and helps create a setting against which a new pastoralism defines itself. The same narrative function is inscribed in the following reflection on the *Westward-Ho!*

version of pastoral escapism: "[T]he country rolls away to the south and the mountains. Where hunters and woodcutters once slept in their boots by the dying light of their thousand fires and went on, old teutonic forebears with eyes incandesced by the visionary light of a massive rapacity, wave on wave of the violent and the insane, their brains stoked with spoorless analogues of all that was, lean aryans with their abrogate semitic chapbook reenacting the dramas and parables therein and mindless and pale with a longing that nothing save dark's total restitution could appease" (4). The passage alludes to the ideas of the Puritan errand into the wilderness, of Manifest Destiny, and of white supremacy. This legacy is identified not just as obsolete but also as pathogenic.

What presents itself in answer to traditional versions of pastoral and in contrast to the gnostic materialism of the city is not a unified ecopastoral alternative. One of several alternative approaches is suggested by Suttree's immersion in nature, and this approach takes its cue from transcendentalism, even in regard to Suttree's failure to become one with the cosmos: Rather than the sublime, he experiences the trivial and the grotesque. Another approach is personified in the Native American Michael who, like Suttree, is a fisherman, and who shares advice, food, secret bait, and a talisman. "As it turns out, Suttree—however he may aspire to it—proves incapable of the kind of oneness with the river which Michael has attained" (Young 105). In a sense, Suttree's mystification over Michael's teachings reflects the role of the Native American worldview as an ecological utopia. A third alternative to traditional pastoral vision is suggested in the treatment of wilderness, and it is the ecopastoral vision that subsumes the other two.

McCarthy's pastoralism is ecopastoral not just because it respects the ecological equality of all creatures and favors undomesticated nature over agricultural land, but, moreover, because it equates the external wilderness of nature with the social wilderness of the city and the internal wilderness of the human mind. As they ignore the distinction that is commonly made between these realms, McCarthy's texts themselves come to function as a narrative wilderness of images and scenes and reflections. In this sense, the interaction of the several modes of wilderness also makes it possible to discuss *Suttree* as if it were in fact a pastoral novel.

Moreover, the equivalence of the several modes of wilderness in the text integrates the picaresque into the pastoral. Without exception, McCarthy's novels contain picaro figures, that is, deracinated protagonists preoccupied with survival more than with lofty quests, and gifted with a comic resourcefulness. Harrogate evidently reveals the trickster-like attributes of the picaro and, in a less comic way, so does Suttree. What matters here is less their identification with this generic role model than the fact that the type of the picaro is allegorically conceived (unlike a realistic character); that the picaresque genre is comic (as opposed to tragic); and that Suttree's quest for survival in an alien cityscape parallels his quest for survival in the Appalachians. Both environments are wild; in neither environment does he care to dominate; and survival in either is equally hard. As if Suttree were in part a "Doomed Huck" (Charyn 14), in part as grandiloquent as Whitman, the novel's ecopastoralism and its picaresque aspects subscribe to the same wilderness ethos.

The egalitarian treatment of society and nature in *Suttree* is two-sided insofar as everything that initially seems meaningless and alien to Suttree later becomes meaningful and inclusive. As if to evoke the proverbial glass of water looking no longer half empty but half full, an angelic boy offers Suttree a drink of water in the final scene. The moment contrasts favorably with Suttree's earlier, grotesque vision of his Saxon forebears who "wait for the waterbearer to come but he does not come, and does not come" (136). Suttree affirms his kinship with the land when he "was struck by the fidelity of this earth he inhabited and he bore it a sudden love" (354).[11] The positive sense of self and place he regains is obviously an extension of his integration into the human environment of his friends, qualifying the trauma of individualized death with the prospect of collective survival. As Vereen Bell argues in regard to the "common cause against the rule of death" in *Suttree,* "This commonality within, which may and should arise from the universality of suffering, is the quid pro quo in human life, brought into life, ironically by death" (*Achievement* 110).

In a way, the survivalist reversal of Suttree's view of life at the novel's end suggests a need to reinterpret the novel's grotesque imagery. For the grotesque, too, is of an egalitarian quality insofar as it is designed to level hierarchies and join incompatible aspects together and to be, above all, infinite, depersonalized, and dynamic. Suttree's dictum "Nothing ever stops moving" (461) captures the anarchic flux at the heart of the grotesque. The grotesque imagery in *Suttree* becomes emblematic of the kind of survivalism that Bakhtin identifies in the grotesque realism of the Renaissance: "The last thing one can say of the real grotesque is that it is static; on the contrary it seeks to grasp in its imagery the very act of becoming and growth, the eternal incomplete unfinished nature of being. Its images present simultaneously the two poles of becoming: that which is receding and dying, and that which is being born; they show two bodies in one, the budding and the division of the living cell. At the summit of grotesque and folklore realism, as in the death of one-cell organisms, no dead body remains" (*Rabelais* 52).

McCarthy's ecopastoralism bespeaks a worldview whose egalitarian underpinnings logically transcend the preference of the pastoral imagination for natural landscape settings. It embraces various modes of narrative discourse, from the loftiest abstraction to the most proletarian idiom. It places philosophical meditations side by side with the most mundane detail. If man is a relative to all living things and is on an existential par with them then civilization represents but one ecosystem among many, and literary discourse yet another. In this sense, every episode and every description in *Suttree* assumes its carefully calculated part in the novel's cosmology. Once McCarthy's aesthetic order is understood, all other aspects begin to fall into place. On this view, all of McCarthy's novels, including *Suttree,* are intrinsically ecopastoral and call for ecocritical readings.

McCarthy's pastoralism defies traditional pastoral approaches because these tend to reduce the pastoral theme to a surface function against which other concerns are played out. McCarthy's pastoralism, however, is inclusive and holistic. The subsequent passage in *Suttree,* for instance, contains the machine-in-the-garden motif, but in a manner that subjects the symbol of intruding industrialism itself to destruction, as if to suggest a shared tendency to entropy while integrating it into the dominant theme of natural beauty. "Wasn't two minutes the whole car was afire. I run to the door and got it open and we was goin up this grade through the mountains in the snow with the moon on it and it was just blue lookin and dead quiet out there and them big old black pine trees going by. I jumped for it and lit in a snowbank and what I'm going to tell you you'll think peculiar but it's the god's truth. That was in nineteen and thirty-one and if I live to be a hunnerd year old I don't think I'll ever see anything as pretty as that train on fire goin up that mountain and around the bend and them flames lightin up the snow and the trees and the night" (182). The slight shifts in focus (from boxcar to door to moonlit snow to pines and back to the receding train), which are effected not through differentiation but through concatenation, result in a nonhierarchical structure that highlights nothing so much as the fact that nothing is highlighted. Man, machine, and nature seem to be in perfect harmony in an aesthetic that is based on the relatedness of things, and not on the incongruity of the machine in the garden. Nowhere in this scene does the train signify industrial intrusion or even contrast with the setting. Instead, the whole scene becomes an emblem of the paradoxical harmony of destruction that informs the savage tableaux of *Outer Dark* and *Blood Meridian* as much as Lester's dream of his last ride in *Child of God* (170–71) or the "miracles of destruction" that the Mormon seeks in *The Crossing* (142).

The parable of the train suggests a pastoral truth that goes beyond the realm of nature to include mankind in shared mortality. Taking the place of the romantic sublime, this vision introduces a metaphysical component in McCarthy's ecopastoralism. The chapters to come will use the term "nature mysticism" to describe this sense of a deeper truth in nature and the integrative function of this mysticism for the texts' sense of pastoral. Whatever is mystical about McCarthy's ecopastoralism ought to be understood as a reference to the experience of the egalitarian essence of the universe, such as described by Whitman in *Specimen Days* as "an intuition of the absolute balance, in time and space, of the whole of this multifarious, mad chaos of fraud, frivolity, hoggishness—this revel of fools, and incredible make-believe and general unsettledness, we call *the world;* a soul-sight of that divine clue and unseen thread which holds the whole congeries of things, all history and time, and all events, however trivial, however momentous, like a leash'd dog in the hand of the hunter" (894). Whitman's dog-and-hunter simile hints at the need for figurative language to describe an essentially ineffable observation. The meaning of the term *animism* in this study—wherever it is applied to describe the ecopastoral ethos in McCarthy's novels—is attendant on this reductive concept of mystical perception, and is in turn to be understood as the conviction that all things animate and inanimate share in existential equality. In short, it is arrived at by way of nature mysticism more than by ecological argument.

The inclusion of an ecocritical angle has become established procedure in McCarthy criticism. The chapters to follow will go a step further and undertake close readings designed to show that McCarthy's work as a whole is crafted according to a unified eco-pastoral aesthetic. McCarthy's novels themselves, in their emphasis on multifaceted structure and semantic interrelationships, affect the complexity of ecosystems. Each textual aspect interrelates with any number of other aspects, and so the analysis of their egalitarianism becomes the most pressing and rewarding task of the McCarthy critic.

CHAPTER ONE

"Beyond the World of Men"

Emergent Ecopastoralism in the Southern Novels

> The solitude and total freedom of the wilderness created a perfect setting for either melancholy or exultation.
>
> Roderick Nash, *Wilderness and the American Mind*

The principal point subsequently argued is that McCarthy's Southern novels already manifest the main components of his later, ecopastoral fiction, such as their melancholy mood, allegorical composition, and ecopastoral genre. The project of *Child of God* can be outlined as departing from the more or less traditional pastoralism of *The Orchard Keeper* while not yet being fully committed to the gothic, self-absorbed anti-pastoralism of *Outer Dark*. Since the pastoral aspects of *The Orchard Keeper* and *Child of God* interrelate closely, and since, moreover, the pastoral aspects of *Outer Dark* anticipate those of *Blood Meridian*, the Southern novels will be discussed in their thematic sequence, rather than in their chronological order.

The Orchard Keeper (1965)

McCarthy's debut novel develops an alternative land ethic that qualifies the nostalgia traditionally associated with pastoralism. Although the pastoral alternative sketched out in *The Orchard Keeper* hardly goes beyond the traditional pastoral elements of escapism, immersion into nature, and defiance of the encroachment of civilization, the text's post-humanist energy combines with melancholy allegoresis to frustrate any superficial classification as elegiac pastoralism.

Among the many instances of allegoresis in *The Orchard Keeper* we find the grave marker described on the penultimate page. The stone marks the grave of the mother of protagonist John Wesley, a boy who grows up fatherless in the Appalachian hamlet of Red Branch, but who is befriended and tutored by Marion Sylder (the man who unwittingly killed his villainous father in self-defense) and by old Arthur Ownby who tends the father's decomposing body without knowing its identity. John Wesley's religiously deluded mother, who once exhorted her teenage son "to find the man that took away your daddy" (66) and swore him in on this task, has passed away during his seven-year absence. She herself remains but a vague impression of "hallucinated recollections" (245) to the young man, evoked by the grave marker's inscription "If thou afflict them in any wise, / And they cry at all unto me, / I will surely hear their cry" (245). The choice of epitaph proves to be meaningful, because the preceding verse in the Bible specifies the beneficiaries of this divine promise: "Ye shall not afflict any widow, or fatherless child" (Exod. 22:23). The verse following that of the inscription specifies the punishment for those who would harm widows or their children, which is quite in line with Mildred Rattner's ideas (the boy's mother): "And my wrath shall wax hot and I will kill you with the sword" (Exod. 22:24).

Yet the entire narrative composition of *The Orchard Keeper* is designed to manifest the vanity of moral constructs such as this one in the context of the natural world. The grave marker becomes emblematic of human hubris on the one hand, and of nature's indifference to human conceits on the other. Although the epitaph is still legible, the grave is about to be overgrown by vegetation, "the stone arrogating to itself in these three short years already a gray and timeless aspect, glazed with lichens and nets of small brown runners, the ring of rusted wire leaning awry against it with its stained and crumpled rags of foliage" (245). In effect, the inscription and the moral paradigm that it represents become allegorical of a gross misrepresentation of the order of things by evoking an unjustified sense of tragedy, an obsolete faith in divine justice and an insistent anthropocentrism. The marker reiterates these notions while not even the one living person it implies, the orphaned John Wesley, cares about them.

Simultaneously, the marker has become an emblem on the coexistence of life and death (verdant vegetation on a grave), of nature's regenerative power (one organism dead, others coming into being), and of cosmic indifference to human morality (erosion of tabled law). John Wesley, seated on the grave and checking his socks, enhances the message of nature's indifference through his own obliviousness, for to him everything the stone commemorates seems "less real than the smell of wood smoke or the taste of an old man's wine" (245). Since his departure seven years earlier, John Wesley appears to have become indifferent to his origins, to the loss of first his father and then his mother, and to the vengeance he swore. His indifference nearly matches that of the lichen overgrowing the tombstone.

Like all of McCarthy's protagonists, John Wesley is a picaresque character, a homeless and parentless figure whose inner life remains undisclosed. Here, at the end of the novel, he seems at peace with a world that is at peace with him. This may seem incongruous for the protagonist of a pastoral novel, and incongruous in the context of the elegiac closing lines of *The Orchard Keeper:* "No avatar, no scion, no vestige of that people remains. On the lips of the strange race that now dwells there their names are myth, legend, dust" (246). These lines appear to contradict the argument for the protagonist's and the text's indifference unless they are read together with the line immediately preceding them that reconfirms the sense of universal equanimity: "Over the land sun and wind still move to burn and sway the trees, the grasses" (246).

The reason for discussing the grave-marker emblem rather than the allegory of tree and fence in the novel's prologue is to argue for an ecocritical revision of conventional pastoral readings that cite the tree allegory for evidence. More than McCarthy's later work, *The Orchard Keeper* has been read in the context of the Faulknerian tradition in Southern pastoralism, what with its rhetorical opulence, structural complexity, and apparent nostalgia for a rustic lifestyle. Intertextual parallels no doubt exist and have been discussed at length,[1] and the novel seems to fit its interpretation as a work of traditional pastoralism so snugly that signs to the contrary may have been overlooked.

That the novel is pastoral in certain respects is undisputed. The novel's very title invokes the pastoral trauma of expropriation elaborated at the end ("They are gone now"), the expulsion from paradise, and the curse on Adam and his kin ("the strange race that now dwells there"), while the prologue insinuates the tree of life cut at the root.[2] The ruined orchard inspires Jerry Leath Mills to liken it to "a fallen Eden" (289), Stanley Trachtenberg to speak of a "prelapsarian Eden" (149), and Dianne C. Luce to call it the novel's "dominant pastoral image" (1). The obscure tank that disrupts the orchard's peacefulness calls to mind Leo Marx's image of the machine in the garden. In short, *The Orchard Keeper* appears to capture that pastoral moment of truth in which things begin to yield to outside intrusion, to shift in "the conflict between tradition and modernity"

(Grammer 30). As it seems "to question the old southern dream of escape from history" (31), Grammer suggests that we read the novel "as an elegy for an older sort of pastoral community, nobly resisting but finally defeated by the Gnostic will to deny history" (35). The novel supports these observations, yet traditional pastoral readings may provide an incomplete understanding. Certain aspects of the text seem to check a conventional pastoral reading.

When William Schafer writes that "the old days and ways have been buried by the weight of change and the present moment" (108), he bases his conclusion on the novel's last paragraph, which states: "They are gone now. Fled, banished in death or exile, lost, undone" (246). In all likelihood, however, this line refers to the principal characters of the novel only (John Wesley, Ownby, and Sylder). Chances are that the old days and ways are not buried at all, because the pastoral realm of the novel is hardly overrun by progress but very much intact. In fact, most threats to the pastoral order are perceived only by Ownby. He is the one to demonize the storage tank into an evil presence conjured up by the dead body in the spray pit. And he himself allows that no one except him might understand his concern, prompting the social worker: "Why not jest up and ast me? . . . Why I done it. Rung shells and shot your hootnanny all to hell?" (221). Even Sylder, who is in most readings identified as another representative of the old values, wonders: "Why was the old man shooting holes in the government tank on the mountain?" (168). In truth, the tank is one old man's personal obsession, and the text says as much when describing the army personnel servicing the tank as "serious and official, but somewhat sleepy and not in any particular hurry" (98), that is, hardly threatening to the rustic order of life.

Other threats materializing in the course of the narrative are equally personal and justifiable by events. What threatens Sylder, for one, is apprehension by the authorities, not civilization's intrusion, and when Sylder is said to have "a bile-sharp foretaste of disaster," he is simply afraid of getting caught: "You sure have got cold feet, she said. He stared up at the dark ceiling. *I'll be damned if I do,* he whispered to himself" (168). Schafer correctly categorizes him as "the classic type of the bandit" who "fights more directly against the men who represent agencies of order and progress" (107). Sylder himself admits the legitimacy of his being wanted, when instructing John Wesley to leave Constable Gifford alone because "[i]t's his job" (213). If later he recants his admonition (214–15), this does not imply that the narrative imagination shares his outlaw perspective but rather that it reflects his personal view of things. It would be hard to argue that Sylder's ethos is idealized in the book, what with his hitting Gifford in the face in his sleep, "the shut fist rocketing down out of blackness and into his face with a pulpy sound like a thrown melon bursting" (167). If anything, it is he who encroaches upon the city with his untaxed liquor and his outlaw morality, he who introduces urban commodities and customs to the village of Red Branch, his machine that invades the garden.

John Wesley, too, is completely absorbed by threats of a personal nature and has maneuvered himself needlessly into delinquency under Sylder's and Ownby's tutelage. From Arthur Ownby comes the book "TRAPPING THE FUR BEARERS OF NORTH AMERICA" (208);[3] from Sylder comes a hunting dog (112); and from his playmates comes the idea to sell the hides of animals for petty cash (207). When John Wesley realizes that selling a dead hawk for bounty is morally questionable, he reacts in a quixotic way, returning the dollar bounty to the courthouse: "I made a mistake, he wadn't for sale" (233). He uses this visit to the county courthouse to verbalize his naive opposition to an ill-understood system (233), then runs away from home over problems for which no one but his mother would have chided him. After revisiting the area, he leaves for good as if to become a drifter like his villainous father or an outlaw like his mentor Sylder, not because of any transformation in the infrastructure of Red Branch. In the much overinterpreted scene at the end of the book,[4] his waving to the unresponsive couple in the car does not signify his alienation from the modern world of traffic but his very familiarity with it, for he waves merely to signal that the lights have changed: "They both looked. The box clicked. He waved to them and the man turned, saw the green light and pulled away" (246). This and other textual evidence suggests that the novel does not seem to be preoccupied with pastoral nostalgia in the traditional sense, but rather with rewriting pastoralism.

A nonconventional reading reveals that *The Orchard Keeper* fosters an incipient ecopastoralism almost before its time. When Trachtenberg writes—in 1965—that "the thematic burden rests with the land itself" (149) he points in this direction, because land or wilderness are in fact the principal protagonists of McCarthy's first novel. Once we have established that the principal commitment of the narrative consciousness is to a certain wilderness perspective, many of the seemingly incompatible components begin to cohere. The "stretches of narrative ruled by no point of view whatever" (Bell, *Achievement* 13), the "subsistence level of feeling and cognition" (Donoghue 5), the "meditative atmosphere" (Ragan 21), the story line of the feral cat: All of these make sense from an ecologically minded perspective.

Moreover, although the novel may contain pastoral nostalgia, its nostalgia fronts for true melancholia, and critics have said so: David Paul Ragan identifies the closing scene as an *ubi sunt* motif (26); Sullivan interprets Ownby's tending of the spray pit as a *memento mori* motif[5] ("Worlds" 722). Death and loss are foregrounded and set into a natural environment, yet the melancholia they inspire does not mourn the passing of the pastoral order, be it of Arcadian or agrarian bent.

Finally, the novel's use of allegory suggests an ecopastoral tendency. Perhaps the primary instance of misread pastoral allegory in *The Orchard Keeper* is the prologue, in which three workers attempt to cut a felled tree into sections but are impeded by an iron fence post overgrown by the tree. The fence encloses the local cemetery—as we learn on the novel's last page—so that the falling tree has figuratively breached the boundary line between the dead and the living. The prologue starts with the words "The tree was down and cut to lengths" and ends as follows:

> He took hold of the twisted wrought-iron, the mangled fragment of the fence, and shook it. It didn't shake. It's growed all through the tree, the man said. We cain't cut no more on it. Damned old elum's bad enough on a saw.
>
> The Negro was nodding his head. Yessa, he said. It most sholy has. Growed all up in that tree. (3)

The figurative meaning of the prologue has generally been understood to signify the hubris of man, who confuses the agency of a living plant with that of a lifeless, man-made tool. Such interpretation—"an odd instance of human vanity as well as ignorance" (Bell, *Achievement* 22)—seems plausible enough, yet the true, allegorical meaning of the prologue seems to be eco-centric; it "has reference to the theme of man and nature interfused" (Bell, *Achievement* 22). The tree is down, felled by man, but it has taken the fence down with it and moreover dulled the instrument of its destruction. Here as elsewhere in the text, the governing principle is the dialectic of death and survival, applied to the cosmos as a whole.

The use of allegory is not restricted to individual motifs such as this one, but extends to the overall composition. So far, the thorough allegorical structuring of *The Orchard Keeper* has gone virtually unnoticed, and this is surprising insofar as some of the narrative aspects make no sense in a purely realistic reading. Among these are the parts dedicated to the description of wildlife, to the setting of the orchard, and to the figure of Ownby. In fact, the notorious opacity of the characters' psychic life and the shifts in point of view can hardly be explained in realistic terms. This is not to say that *The Orchard Keeper* is structured like a pure parable—the way *Outer Dark* is—but that to ignore the allegorical composition of the novel may imply a misreading. Allegorical and mimetic narrations are not incompatible, because allegorical discourse operates through discursive striation and is careful in constructing a realistic surface narrative that opens onto a meta-narrative (as, for instance, in a fable). Realism in allegorical writing transcends the purposes of mimesis "since the more the allegorist can circumscribe the attributes, metonymic and synecdochic, of his personae, the better he can shape their fictional destiny" (Fletcher 199). Showing that some of McCarthy's figures are types more than realistically developed characters would therefore help explain why "McCarthy's people have virtually no memory and no power of conceptual intelligence" (Aldridge 91), why "they meet the world without the mediation of law, morality, religion, or politics" (Donoghue 5), and why "these people are never seen from within" (Prescott L45). John Aldridge implies as much when arguing that "if the absence of plot represents a violation of one Aristotelian law, it does obey another—that of decorum or truth to type" (91). The truth is that the aesthetic complexity of *The Orchard Keeper* can hardly be grasped without understanding its typological underpinnings.

Commenting on the text's "paucity of narrative structure—either conventional or experimental" (296), Mark Winchell observes that "McCarthy so consistently avoids the transitions and connections of a well-made novel that we suspect neither accident nor ineptitude but some more insidious design to be at work" (295). He goes on to suggest that the narration of *The Orchard Keeper* proceeds in an illogical, nonlinear, unstructured way, that it frustrates the reader's expectation as to conventional plotting, and that this apparent lack of narrative organization may well be intended. But these findings translate into a cogent and fine-tuned strategy that operates with analogy (variation of form but not of content), type (variation of person but not of character), and fable (variation of surface story but not of underlying plot). These features are hallmarks of allegorical writing, which proceeds paratactically rather than hypotactically and in a cyclical rather than a linear way.

When Donoghue observes that all actions in McCarthy's novels are connected by "and," "not by and then and then and then" (5), he is in fact describing the technique of parataxis, used in allegoresis. Fletcher specifies that the term parataxis "implies a structuring of sentences such that they do not convey any distinctions of higher or lower order. 'Order' here means intensity of interest, since what is more important usually gets the greater share of attention. In parataxis each predication stands alone" (162). This procedure defines McCarthy's style: a mosaic of self-contained elements, "a multitude of scenes, often loosely affiliated or not at all" (Donoghue 5). In the following quote, each incident can be seen to be equidistant from the narrative perspective: "He was pushing time now and he could feel it give. She canned the remainder of the garden in two days and was after him to get his bed back up to the loft before he took cold. It rained and the pond went blood-red and one afternoon he caught a bass from the willows in water not a foot deep and cleaned it and held the tiny heart in the palm of his hand, still beating" (65–66). Here, the narrative focus shifts from John Wesley to his mother, to the weather, to fishing, and to death. The narrator sets the image of the dying bass beside the change of season and the concerns of housekeeping and growing up, as if to make them seem existentially equivalent.

Comparable to the visual effect of still lives, the narrative effect of parataxis is essentially that of *vanitas* imagery: allegorical and melancholy in its ceaseless reference to mortality and the transience of secular achievement. The rhythmic leveling of differences expresses the indifference of the melancholy mind, while the repeated enunciation of this indifference itself prescribes meaning and order where none seemed to exist before. Parataxis thereby assumes an incantatory quality in its very repetitiveness, like a ritual chant meant to drown out the sorrow it articulates. The following quote not only forgoes the use of causal conjunctions and proper grammar, but dwindles to a line of dots in one place: "Silence now in the houses. Repose. Even to those for whom no end of night could bring rest enough. And silence, the music fled in seeping amber warmth of innumerable dreams laid to death upon the hearth, ghostly and still . . . The morning is yet to the nether end of the earth, and he is weary. Bowing the grass in like sadness the dew followed him home and sealed his door" (67). As the last line confirms, nature partakes of human sorrow in the novel's allegorical vision. A similar narrative form with the same effect is the doubling of plot, also found in the novel. It is exemplified by Ownby's radical departures: He gives up his settled life when his wife elopes, he gives it up again when the sheriff comes for him, and he is made to give it up a third time when Agent Huffaker arrests him. Another instance of plot doubling is represented by the story of the stray cat, whose predatory drifting parallels the progress of Kenneth Rattner (John Wesley's father) earlier in the book. Both the cat and Rattner are alien presences wherever they go, both are scavengers, both die violent deaths at the hand of a superior predatory being, and the link between them is explicitly established by Ownby. When he learns that Mr. Eller heard a cat scream overhead as it is borne away by an owl (217), he explains, "Lots of times that happens, a body dies and their soul takes up in a cat for a spell. Specially somebody drownded or like that where they don't get buried proper" (227). He associates the captured cat with Rattner's soul, which he feels is "bound most probably for hell" (228), while the narrator uses the words "unburied remains" (91) in reference to Rattner's body.

Among other things, the subplots of Rattner and the cat are narrated with an equal degree of contempt, their deaths reported with the same sense of relief. The allegorical type they represent is that of the *pharmakon,* that is, the scapegoat creature in Greek mythology, who contaminates the community, and whose sacrificial death induces a collective catharsis.[6] Rattner's presence not only determines the shamanistic function of Ownby's covering of his body but also identifies Ownby as the arbiter of the novel's morality. Although it may seem as if the novel's plot could do without these two figures, the parallels between them signal a deeper collusion and inform their existence with narrative necessity for the allegorical level of the text. The narrative strategy of disguising humans as animals is familiar from the allegorical genre of the fable, while the fact that two parallel stories are told, one character being human, one animal, suggests yet again an ecopastoral aspect: The animal world and the human world are rolled into one.

A third, ecocritically inspired, multiplication of plots concerns the hunting theme. Analogies abound between the she-panther hunting for her baby in Ownby's tale, Ownby being out hunting while Rattner is killed, John Wesley hunting his father's killer (if only in his mother's fantasy), Sylder hunting together with friends and John Wesley, John Wesley trapping, Constable Gifford hunting John for trapping out of season, the stray cat hunting for John's trapped prey, the owl hunting the stray cat, and cats hunting Ownby (in his fantasy). Although the hunting incidents are isolated and self-contained, they link the characters (again both human and animal) in a cycle of hunting and being hunted, death being the ultimate huntsman. The narrative attitude toward hunting is a melancholy one, with the narrator manifesting sorrow over the fact of death. This is important because the melancholy aspect subsumes the redoubling plotlines under the theme of pastoral melancholia. Evidence in support of this theory can be found among the subchapters devoted to the hunting tales in the third part of the text, in which a dead owl is presented as a *memento mori* image: "From a lightwire overhead, dangling head downward and hollowed to the weight of ashened feathers and fluted bones, a small owl hung in an attitude of forlorn exhortation, its wizened talons locked about the single strand of wire. It stared down from dark and empty sockets, penduluming softly in the bitter wind" (143). The dead owl is beheld by Ownby, and once again his and the narrator's perspective overlap in joint melancholia. The recurrence of the hunting motif suggests ritual reiteration in order to come to terms with the realization that everybody may in turn be hunter and prey. Similarly, the snake killed for its rattles functions as an emblem of this ambiguity (201).

Other instances of the melancholy theme revolve around a "pattern of entrapment or containment" (Luce 8) that shows animals caught in human structures. One such instance involves the rabbit that John Wesley finds in the well and feeds until it dies. More interesting, however, is the paragraph preceding this event: "The well hidden in the weeds and johnson grass that burgeoned rankly in the yard had long shed its wall of rocks and they were piled in the dry bottom in layers between which rested in chance interment the bones of rabbits, possums, cats, and other various and luckless quadrupeds" (63). The melancholia of this moment, and the death of the rabbit in the following paragraph, intensifies the cautioning intent of the *et in Arcadia ego* motif[7] until it signifies full-blown sorrow, as if to suggest that death represents the governing principle of existence. Read ecocritically, such scenes imply that wildlife and civilization are incompatible, and that therefore any truce between the two, let alone harmony, is illusory. The recurrent mention of this incompatibility, then, points to the ecopastoral commitment of the novel.

The most conspicuous doubling of plot structures surfaces in the use of seasonal and numerological cycles. Thus, the four parts of the novel correspond to the passing seasons, from summer to spring. The Green Fly Inn burns on the winter solstice of 1936 (47), and it is on the winter solstice of each year that Ownby covers Rattner's body with cedar boughs (131, 138). The main plot action covers a seven-year span from 1934 to 1941, John Wesley is gone for another seven years, his father's body is tended seven years in the spray pit, and Ownby counts history in cycles of seven. In effect, the recurrent mention of cyclical events suggests a typological view of history, comparable to that of Christian historiography. Small wonder that the cyclical changes of nature that Ownby teaches John Wesley sound biblical: "[T]he old man explained that there was a lean year and a year of plenty every seven years" (225–26).

Ownby's belief implies an antiprogressive perspective that rejects the teleology of the dominant culture. As it replaces historiographic explanation with concatenation of identical events, Ownby's typological concept of history reformulates the denial of history that has been the hallmark of pastoral escapism. Not just Ownby but also the narrator of *The Orchard Keeper* see the seven-year cycles as repetitions of the cycles of lean and fat years that Joseph outlines for Pharaoh, and all cycles in the novel are allegorical of a cyclical history. The description of the spring floods contains the following image: "Fenceposts like the soldiers of Pharaoh marched from sight into the flooded draws" (173). Elsewhere, a litter of diseased kittens is said to look "as if they might have been struck simultaneously with some biblical blight" (180), and both instances refer again to the story of the Israelites in Egypt. The typological chronicling of events in reference to antecedent events, matching them in importance and magnitude, suggests an epic sense of time. Together with the theme of natural cycles and seasonal changes it implies a belief in fate while minimizing the influence of human agency on the course of things.

The recurrent mention of natural disasters matches the destructive aspect of civilization with an equally savage onslaught by nature, as if Red Branch was under joint siege. Read as a theme, the recurrence of natural disasters attains a retaliatory aspect: nature striking back. Allusions to natural disasters are found throughout the text: "[A] final desolation seemed to come, as if on the tail of the earth's last winter a well of water were rising slowly up through the very universe itself" (179). Another premonition of disaster is verbalized by Ownby: "I look for this to be a bad one. I look for real calamity afore this year is out" (225). The year is 1941, and the attack on Pearl Harbor just before "this year is out" will plunge the nation into a war as calamitous as the biblical deluge. In the description of Red Branch the houses look "transient and happenstantial as if set there by the recession of floodwaters" and "[s]ome terrible plague seemed to overtake them one by one" (11), whereas their tenants looked like "the victims of some terrible disaster, and stared out across the blighted land" (12). A hailstorm is likened to "a plague of ice" (171). Legwater sifts through Rattner's ashes with "a fevered look in his eye like some wild spodomantic sage divining in driven haste the fate of whole galaxies against their imminent ruin" (240). Even the closing image of *The Orchard Keeper* is catastrophic, describing "the darkening headland drawing off the day, heraldic, pennoned in flame, the fleeing minions scattering their shadows in the wake of the sun" (246).

The intention of this narrative procedure is egalitarian, and by inference ecopastoral. In placing human violence, for example, on a par with violence in nature and likening both to the indiscriminate violence of blind fate, *The Orchard Keeper* assigns equal existential standing to things, animals, and humans: "The lives of men and animals enclose each other, until the disparate orbits are seen as concentric, worlds within worlds" (Schafer 108). In his one monologue on his view of the world, Ownby formulates the interrelatedness of climate, wildlife, and humans: "Get older, he said, you don't need to count. You can read the signs. You can feel it in your ownself. Knowed a blind man oncet could tell lots of things afore they happent. But it'll be hot and dry. Late frost is one sign if you don't know nothin else. So they won't but very little make because folks thinks that stuff grows by seasons and it don't. It goes by weather. Game too, and folks themselves if they knowed it" (225). Using parataxis, cycles and typology, *The Orchard Keeper* subverts the anthropocentrism that is essential in pastoral fiction to create an ideal realm that is a compromise between urban civilization and undomesticated wilderness. Without the separation and distinction between what is human and what is nonhuman, or, to be more precise, without the dogma of human stewardship of creation (as proposed in Genesis 1:28), the pastoral idea loses its meaning.

As this non-anthropocentric cosmology erases the normative status of civilization for the narrative, it puts in its place an animistic universe conceived along ecological lines (coexistence in the same biosphere). To establish this animistic worldview, *The Orchard Keeper* again uses an allegorical device, to wit, the projection of an alternative cosmos. Creating an allegorical microcosm in loose analogy to the real-life macrocosm—and rendering it subject to discursive manipulation—is the technique of parable and fable. In *The Orchard Keeper,* the title confers such an allegorical role onto the orchard: Referring back to the garden of Eden as a place of ideal (because divine) order in nature (the idea of the old pastoralism), this orchard abandoned by man and reclaimed by nature becomes the intratextual microcosm in which a new pastoralism is outlined. Unsurprisingly, the majority of scenes surround the orchard or its immediate environs: Much of Sylder's, much of John Wesley's, and practically all of Ownby's story line have their setting here.

Far from being a sentimental commemoration of a lost Eden, the title *The Orchard Keeper* represents an aesthetic program, an emblem that is subject to reinterpretation. Accordingly, the figurative meaning of the title confers the role of an allegorical guardian upon Ownby, whose mission is to protect the world of the orchard through an ecologically minded counter-magic.[8] For the pastoral context and the allegorical meta-text, Ownby represents the principal protagonist. Most reviews of the novel treat John Wesley as the main protagonist because he seems to provide the point of view more often than the other two protagonists.[9] But actually, John Wesley's point of view governs twenty-four subchapters against

Ownby's twenty-eight (three of these subchapters being shared by both). Apart from his textual prominence, the novel's title and essence link Ownby with the narrative perspective. Not only does he clearly represent the pastoral conscience in *The Orchard Keeper,* the text also allows for a relatively high degree of insight into his psyche by including stream-of-consciousness flashbacks and other reminiscences, his fears, his dreams, his meditations, and finally his prophecies.

Ownby can hardly be said to be mediating between wilderness and civilization from a classical pastoral position. Although Ownby may fill a traditional pastoral role in his avuncular tutelage of John Wesley, and although his shotgun assault on the storage tank may represent a traditional reaction against outside intrusion, the object of his "ecological and cultural defiance" (Luce 4) is hardly the preservation of the pastoral middle ground. Instead, the text establishes Ownby's pastoral status biographically as a progressive immersion into wilderness. This development begins with the failure of his yeoman existence and ends with his retreat into the wilderness (his full commitment to a primitivist pastoralism). In effect, his apparent defiance seems to be motivated not so much by impotent rage against, or misanthropic grief over, the human destruction of pastoral space, as by a mystical primitivism whose agenda includes defiance and escapism. Hence, understanding Ownby provides the key to the nascent ecopastoralism of *The Orchard Keeper.*

Details of Ownby's personal past are provided in the tall tale of the "painters" that he tells John Wesley and his friends, and by occasional memory flashbacks throughout the narrative. What is reported in these fragmentary memories suggests that Ownby has not always lived in tune with nature and has resented outside invasion of pastoral space; has not always been a recluse living off the land; has not always been susceptible to supernatural phenomena. Young Warn Pulliam relates that "[h]im and Grandaddy Pulliam worked together cutting sleepers for the K S & E" (145); Ownby himself mentions that as "a young feller" he was "workin on the road crew," and that in the line of this work "we was blastin" (151), that is, he used dynamite to cut through a mountainside. In other words, he himself actively furthered human encroachment upon wild nature in the past by working for a railroad company and in road construction. Shooting a "crude X across the face of the tank" (97) in the narrative present testifies to the fact that his acceptance of progress has turned into violent opposition since the days of his youth, implying not a simple change of mind, but a change of character.

The key to this change of attitude lies in Ownby's idealism. At some point he appears to have tried his hand at a modest yeoman existence, bought and farmed a small homestead "five mile this side of Sevierville," and aspired to the agrarian ideal of pastoralism: "I had bought me a place off a man named Delozier—twenty acres, mostly side-hill and not much of a house neither, a old piece of a barn . . . I was married then and that was my first place so I reckon I was kindly what you might say proud of it. I kep some hogs and chickens and later on I had me a cow and a wore-out mule, put me in some corn . . . I never had nothin, ain't got nothin now, but I figured it was a start. I wadn't a whole lot older'n you fellers, nineteen, I think I was" (152). What the boys get from Ownby here is a tall tale, folksy and funny; but what the reader gets in the form of the interspersed flashback passages is Ownby's recollection of how he lost his wife, property, and livelihood. As it relates to his reaction to his wife Ellen's elopement with a Bible salesman, this secondary tale overlaying the first contains an allegory on the death of Ownby's pastoral dream: "He stayed for five more days, wandering about the house or sitting motionless, sleeping in chairs, eating whatever he happened to find until there wasn't any more and then not eating anything. While the chickens grew thin and the stock screamed for water, while the hogs perished to the last shoat. An outrageous stench settled over everything, a vile decay that hung in the air, filled the house" (155). The excerpt describes his catatonic reaction to a devastating loss. It marks the onset of Ownby's lifelong melancholia, because the sorrow he experienced forms his sense of self. Far from forgotten, this memory erupts during the storytelling episode and on other occasions. After losing his wife, and being shot in his attempt to reclaim her (92, 230), Ownby "stopped going to work" (155). He seems to have been forced to sell his place to settle a debt (156), and thus to have lost everything. The experience marks the turning point in Ownby's life in several respects, including his sense of pastoral.[10]

On the surface, the episode identifies Ownby as a romantic because the loss of his love appears to precipitate a dejection of such intensity that he will never recover from it. He will never engage in either romance or animal husbandry again. The retrospective within the episode reveals that personal loss has driven him out of doors to lead the life of a recluse. Arguably then, the ruin of his homestead is brought about not by gross neglect or even shock but by the self-destructive impulse of his melancholy psyche. The violence of letting his livestock perish (implicating it in his own loss or Ellen's elopement) is directed more against Ownby's own ego than against the beasts, for it copies the destruction of his pastoral and romantic self (155). As Ownby loses faith in the possibility of romantic fulfillment, he also loses his faith in a yeoman existence in tune with the land.

Ownby's personal sadness thus becomes allegorical of a deeper melancholia over the lost origin in, or harmony with, nature. To Ownby's melancholy gaze, a recovery of the continuity of man with nature has become tantamount to attaining the continuity of death. It is a psychoanalytical commonplace to associate romance with death as variations of a continuity that encompasses the forces of both Eros and Thanatos. That Ownby does indeed link libidinal desire with death becomes evident when he remembers how he once refused to join his friends to look at a naked woman. "One night taking a shortcut they passed a house and saw through one window a woman undressing for bed. The others had gone back *for a second look* but he would not go and they laughed at him. The old man remembered it now with dim regret, and remembered such nights when the air was warm as a breath and the moon no dead thing. He started down the road to the orchard path and to the pit *for this second look*" (89; emphases added). The second use of the phrase "second look" refers to a check on the body decomposing in the spray pit, but it explicitly reconnects also to the earlier sight of a woman undressing.

Ownby's melancholy fascination with death and loss becomes clearer in the context of another instant close to the novel's end: "and the old man felt the circle of years closing, the final increment of the curve returning him again to the inchoate, the prismatic flux of sound and color wherein he had drifted once before and now beyond the world of men" (222). Here, the projection of the continuity of death and the afterworld marks Ownby again as a melancholy subject. Most important, the vision of this continuity is conspicuously repeated at the very end of the novel, articulated this time by the narrator in a *vanitas* motif and verifying that the narrative perspective ties in with Ownby's. "The dead sheathed in the earth's crust and turning the slow diurnal of the earth's wheel, at peace with eclipse, asteroid, the dusty novae, their bones brindled with mold and the celled marrow going to frail stone, turning, their fingers laced with roots, at one with Tut and Agamemnon, with the seed and the unborn" (244–45). The parallel to the previous quote is obvious: Here as there, cosmic continuity is associated with the prenatal and the posthumous state; subjective identity is erased. Bell similarly identifies the theme of continuity and interprets the passage to mean "that our human status in the world is provisional and that our genuinely enduring continuity with it is ironically inhuman, elemental, and complete" (*Achievement* 10).

By contrast, the nostalgia of older versions of pastoral, caused by the realization that human mortality and historical progress are inescapable, simply mourns the impossibility of pastoral fulfillment. It does not mourn the demise of nature altogether, nor do older idealizations of wilderness.[11] The motif of wilderness destruction appears, for instance, in *The Pioneers* (1823), in which Cooper indicts the careless exploitation of nature in the great fishing episode, the pigeon shooting, and the figure of wasteful Bill Kirby. It also enters into Faulkner's *Go Down Moses* (1942) and *Light in August* (1932) in the clear-cutting of forests. But outside baroque allegoresis, nature itself has never been considered subject to mortality. Rather, it was assumed that man, who effected the destruction of wilderness, would be able to check his past mismanagement of nature by exercising prudence in the future. So the skepticism of urban civilization, the escape from the city and into the wild for a revitalizing experience of nature's sublimity, and even the warning against the disappearance of wilderness have been familiar themes in pastoral writing. But the idea of human stewardship of the earth remained more or less uncontested up to the relatively recent "shift of allegiance toward the antitechnocratic, pastoral mentality prefigured by many of the writers whose work we have canonized as 'classic' American literature" (Marx, "Pastoralism" 39). Recent ecopastoralism—though equally escapist, romantic, utopian—no longer idealizes a "via media" of man in harmony with nature on human terms, but post-humanist harmony with nature based on an ecological equilibrium.

The two emblems of continuity quoted earlier (one being

Ownby's premonition of death, the other the narrator's reflection on the decomposition of the human body) suggest a post-humanist impulse that draws on the old *et in Arcadia ego* motif but transcends it. The *et in Arcadia ego* motif has served to allegorize the intrusion of death into the pastoral realm as a presence that no society can escape. By contrast, the two quotes from *The Orchard Keeper* concerning human continuity with both nature and death represent a radical departure from traditional American pastoralism because the melancholy gaze of Ownby and the narrator—while admittedly a narrative conceit—joins man and nature in the continuity of a shared materiality and cyclical regeneration, if at the cost of divesting man of individual identity. Ownby's recognition of nature's mortality is paraphrased in Love's observation that "until recently, the fate of the individual human soul was played out against a setting of natural grandeur and certainty. Now, it is the death of that conception of nature itself that troubles our pastoral dreams" (201).

In sum, the novel's rejection of civilization is introduced by a narrative sleight. On the one hand, *The Orchard Keeper* uses pastoral allegory as a narrative vehicle to communicate a melancholia that invalidates the idea of human supremacy in view of human mortality and nature's indifferent materiality. On the other hand, the leveling gaze of this melancholia couches a materialist worldview in pastoral allegory. Finally, the very articulation of Ownby's sorrow and his wilderness mysticism serves as an antidote against the narrator's own melancholia.

Within the larger perspective, these aspects of Ownby's character correspond to elements on the meta-narrative level.[12] The correspondence not only confirms Ownby's role as the avatar of the novel's sense of pastoral, it also provides a larger context for Ownby's wilderness ethic. Most prominent among those of Ownby's character traits communicated by the overall narrative are a non-teleological view of history, an underlying melancholy mood (including the preoccupation with death), and faith in the regenerative powers of wilderness (regenerating not the woodsman, but nature itself). Evidence of this wilderness perspective is given early in the novel by the images of wild vegetation, juxtaposed with the "parched and sere" crops standing "in defeat" under an "infernal sky": "In the relative cool of the timber stands, possum grapes and muscadine flourish with a cynical fecundity, and the floor of the forest—littered with old mossbacked logs, peopled with toadstools strange and solemn among the ferns and creepers and leaning to show their delicate livercolored gills—has about it a primordial quality, some steamy carboniferous swamp where ancient saurians lurk in feigned sleep" (11). Like Ownby, the narrative voice does not decry the desolation of the pastoral realm but celebrates wilderness wherever it reclaims space from man. In the passage below, the wounded hawk combines the aspect of mortality with the invincible spirit of wilderness (a topic that McCarthy picks up again in the contexts of the moribund wolf in *The Crossing* and the extinction of wolves in *Cities of the Plain*): "It was in August that he had found the sparrowhawk on the mountain road, crouched in the dust with one small falcon wing fanned and limp, eying him without malice or fear—something hard there, implacable and ungiving. It followed his movements as he approached and then turned its head when he reached out his hand to it, picked it up, feeling it warm and palpitant in the palm of his hand, not watching him, not moving, but only looking out over the valley calmly with its cold-glinting accipitral eyes, its hackles riffling in the wind" (77). This language feeds on the same melancholy energy that invests the moment of Ownby's arrest. He, too, looks into the distance in sudden realization of imminent loss:[13] "The old man had stopped. He was looking at the man, and then he was looking past him, eyes milk-blue and serene, studying the dipping passage of a dove, and beyond, across the canted fields of grass to the green mountain, and to the thin blue peaks rising into the distant sky with no crestline of shape or color to stop them, ascending forever" (202). In the words "ascending forever" the discrepancy between nature's continuity and Ownby's own finite existence becomes painfully apparent, and the narrator endorses the mood. As elsewhere in McCarthy's fiction, the melancholia is linked to the sense of loss of pastoral vision even, and especially, on the meta-narrative plane.

Rather than giving itself over to pastoral lament, however, *The Orchard Keeper* tempers the loss by renegotiating the pastoral quest as an alliance between the pastoral mentality and the materiality of wilderness, and by creating an allegorical figure endowed with a supernatural sensibility for the complexity of wilderness. Luce argues that "in *The Orchard Keeper,* as in the Border Trilogy, the vanquishing of the orchard is presented without ecological despair: *The Orchard Keeper* evokes the persistence of the natural world despite the vanishing human generations and the ruin of their material artifacts" (8). The concluding scenes of *The Orchard Keeper,* while marked by decay and melancholia, arguably favor tranquillity of mind over pastoral nostalgia. The ecopastoral alliance between protagonist and nature is suggested not just by Ownby's temporary withdrawal into the wilderness of the "harrykin" but also in John Wesley's westward departure. And so the assumption that the representatives of the old pastoralism may have gone, "banished or in exile" (246), implies nothing so much as a new escapism, a continued pastoral hope.

In this way, *The Orchard Keeper* anticipates McCarthy's ecopastoral shift in the Border Trilogy and its evolution of an initially optimistic, then increasingly skeptical, utopianism. Tim Poland associates ecopastoralism with Western, not Southern, writing because "in much western literature, the usual relationship between character and landscape is inverted. Rather than a landscape that exists as setting for human action and is imprinted with human qualities, the landscape in much western writing functions more like a character in itself and imprints on the human characters its own qualities" (197). Perhaps this quality of the Western landscape caused McCarthy to move his settings from the South to the Southwest after *Suttree.* But as early as *The Orchard Keeper* he foregrounds nature as a character in its own right (in just the way Poland outlines).

Child of God (1973)

It is sensible to skip *Outer Dark* for the time being and to discuss *Child of God,* the third novel, in conjunction with *The Orchard Keeper* because *Child of God* seeks to represent wilderness in a narrative mode largely uncompromised by a pastoral perspective, a tendency suggested but not fully realized in *The Orchard Keeper.* It is a novel about wilderness inside and out, or, to be more precise, a representation of wild nature as reflected in a psyche gone wild. Some of the changes from *The Orchard Keeper* to *Child of God* are obvious even without concrete textual substantiation. For instance, *Child of God* is strongly devoted to representing the beauty of nature, but it forgoes the use of the elegiac tone that *The Orchard Keeper* still manifests in respect to a defunct ideal of rusticity. *Child of God* does contain the theme of escapism, if without the ecstatic sense of withdrawal from civilization and immersion into nature. It features important tenets of pastoralism such as self-reliance, autonomy, and individualism but reduces them to pathological distortions or rudiments of themselves. The polarity between urban and rural environments is nominally preserved (though Sevierville hardly represents the city), but the middle landscape is actually made to stand in stark opposition to raw wilderness, with aesthetic preference given to the latter. As Jarrett notes, the novel's landscape "is no pastoral scene but a primal wilderness bereft of human order" (41). Wilderness proceeds here to replace the middle landscape as the most meaningful pastoral space.

It might be too simple to categorize *Child of God* as "antipastoral" (Bartlett 14) and see mere parody where McCarthy offers innovative, contemporary answers to some of the fundamental problems plaguing the pastoral genre. These problems revolve around the figure of the pastoral protagonist, one being the dilemma that the pastoral protagonist has to combine the simplicity of his barely developed environment and his rustic profession with a poet's sophistication and elocution. Another is that any pastoralism is marred by the discrepancy between the silent materiality of nature and the communicative intention of art. A third dilemma is the conflict between narrative action and narrative vision: The more a given pastoral protagonist *does* to propel the plot progression, the less he *sees* and expands the discursive appreciation of nature. Finally, there is the wilderness-turn in contemporary pastoralism itself, which is problematic because an environment defined as not-human is to be represented in its own right, without becoming anthropomorphous and romanticized.

Child of God responds to these dilemmas with a unity of form and content that transcends the conceptual scope and ambition of McCarthy's debut novel. If nothing else, the argument to follow will disprove Bell's contention that the novel contains "an unusual degree of unassimilated raw material" (*Achievement* 53). A closer look at the complexity of *Child of God* will both assimilate the raw material and show that the central objective of the novel is the narrative representation of wilderness, strangely mediated by the deranged (and therefore aesthetically conditioned) vision of a farmer who has reverted to the condition of a hunter-gatherer.

The insights gained by such interpretation are as follows: First, *Child of God* has to be understood as an intrinsically pastoral novel, concerned throughout with the non-humanized representation of undomesticated nature. The narrative device used to effect this form of representation is the largely unreflected, primitive, if faintly articulate, point of view of a man who has turned into a pathological predator, that is, the perspective of a virtual savage to communicate a more authentic representation of wilderness.

Second, in stylizing the psychopathic protagonist as a "throwback representative of Rousseau's natural man" (Jarrett 40–41) McCarthy is rewriting the American pastoral type of the frontiersman, of the American Adam, whose formative experience is regeneration through the confrontation with, and survival in, the American wilderness. In a grotesque way, Lester Ballard reconnects to antecedent figures of American pastoralism, such as Natty Bumppo, Daniel Boone, Kit Carson, Melville's Ishmael, or even Thoreau.

Third, the purpose of this literary undertaking, on the metanarrative level, is to move the pastoral protagonist further toward the wilderness. The novel tries to relocate him at the interstice between the middle landscape and wilderness, or, to be more precise, between the realms of man and not-man. Lester's status as both social outcast and psychotic renegade exempts him, wherever his vision provides the point of view, from the qualifying gaze of the plot-level community, until the wildness within matches the wilderness without.

At issue, finally, is not (simply) pastoral nostalgia articulated by a representative of the middle landscape (as is the case in *The Orchard Keeper*) but a contemporary concern with the aesthetic representation of wilderness, that is, a concern with a "primitive" aesthetic of nature that is indebted to the transcendentalist pastoralism of *Walden* while being rooted in present-day materialism and Southern gothicism.

Taken individually, these propositions hardly seem original. Taken together, however, they suggest a more comprehensive approach to the novel. Many discussions of *Child of God* concentrate on individual angles, such as the psyche of Lester Ballard, the novel's use of vernacular, or the pastoral theme in a traditional sense. Pastoral interpretations tend to read the plot as a dramatization of Southern society in microcosm, and liken the novel to a fable on failed Jeffersonian agrarianism in general and the Southern denial of history in particular. Such readings are supported by the opening scene (the foreclosure auction of the Ballard estate), by the subsequent disenfranchisement of the protagonist, by the elegiac pastoral scene on pages 169 and 170, and by the scene of Ballard's reemergence from the caves (190). Validated by the use of the vernacular and the patent emphasis on landscape description, this kind of pastoral reading need not go any deeper.

Just as in the case of *The Orchard Keeper,* the problem with a straight pastoral reading is that it diagnoses the text as an elegy for the defunct pastoral order of the middle landscape, even though this environment is shown to be in perfect order. Far from being invaded by industrialism, Lester's farm is simply taken over by a more ambitious landholder, John Greer, who seems to run it at a profit. Lester himself squats, for a while, on the land of another successful farmer, Waldrop, who takes no action against Lester even after he runs his nephew off (94), shoots one of his cows (34), and finally burns down the abandoned cabin he occupied (104–105). The tableau of husbandman and team (169–70) comes across as nostalgic not because it forms an irredeemable part of the past (it does not), but because Lester, who observes the team's progress, has willfully forfeited his claim to an agrarian existence. Even the blacksmith miniature (70–74) does not commemorate a bygone order of things but pays homage to craftsmanship and a certain work ethos, though this is clearly lost on Lester. Finally, the redemptive episode of Lester's return to the state hospital confirms, more than it mourns, the continued existence of the pastoral order as realized in the backwoods of Tennessee: "In April of that same year a man named Arthur Ogle was plowing an upland field" (195).

The novel's compositional unity of structure and iconography suggests an inclusive pastoral reading that identifies the novel's narrative achievement—beyond the pastoral storytelling, beyond the community portrait, and beyond the psychograph of Lester—as a reorientation of the pastoral perspective toward wilderness (rather than the imaginary garden), toward the primitive mind (rather than the philosophical mind), toward survival (rather than the recovery of vitality and virtue), and toward equality (rather than stewardship). Ultimately, the text reveals a narrative consciousness as preoccupied with the representation of nature's beauty as it is plagued by the realization of nature's indifference to man.

The novel's complexity becomes already apparent in the careful structuring of the narrative progression. Lester's story is determined by the circular movement of the traditional pastoral plot. Marx typifies the pastoral plotline as a succession of three stages, the first of which describes the protagonist's flight from civilization, his "disengagement from a social environment felt to be excessively constraining, complex, hierarchical, ordered, alienating" ("Pastoralism" 55) as he yields to the escapist impulse. In the second, central stage, the protagonist embarks on his quest for a "realm 'closer' to nature in search of freedom and independence or, in effect, the basis for a simpler, more natural way of life" (55–56). The third stage marks his return and reconciliation with the order he fled. The impulse to return is triggered by "an often traumatic and finally chastening encounter with wildness" during which the protagonist realizes the "indifference and immensity of Not-Man" (57). In *Child of God,* this three-stage model defined by Marx appears to be borne out by the subdivision of the novel into three parts.[14] One could loosely summarize part 1 as establishing the rural setting and its social environment, introducing its freakish protagonist and relating the foreclosure of his property and his eviction. Part 2 chronicles his growing alienation; his withdrawal first into an abandoned cabin, then completely outdoors; his progressive derangement; and his transgression into lawlessness and crime. Part 3 is marked by an anticlimactic change of tone, as it returns the broken protagonist to the community of man and redeems him in the eyes of his fellow beings and the narrator. If part 1 is thematically defined by the experience of pastoral loss, then part 2 is devoted to the quest for a frontier livelihood—however quixotic it may be—while reintegration and pastoral redemption are the defining themes of part 3.

Analogously, the narrative structure of the first part is dominated by the idiomatic banter and tall tales characterizing the literary tradition of Southern humor and rustic storytelling: Its form is episodic and dialogic; its imagery comic; its language ironic, of oral quality; it has the community focus of most folklore. Part 2 shows formal parallels to a crime story and is dominated by progressive plot action, realistic detail, and gothic iconography. In part 3, the form changes to narrative reflection and speculation, meditative or lyrical diction, nature and dream imagery.[15] The narrative perspective shifts from privileging a zero-level point of view that integrates, and thus implicates, the reader in the exchange of Lester-lore, to the predominance of third-person narration from

Lester's point of view in the central part, to the omniscient perspective of the narrator who accesses and interprets Lester's state of mind with the benefit of hindsight in the later part of the book.

The progressive intensification of narrative insight, however, runs contrary to the story's chronology. The opening scene constitutes a straightforward piece of prose clearly set in the past, and it creates unease on the part of the reader, perhaps premonitory of escalating violence. But with the second subchapter commences the first of the oral testimonies, whose point of narration is located in the present, not the past. Not until far into the book does the reader know enough to realize that the comical Lester mythology is created posthumously, in full knowledge of Lester's crimes. The reader, still ignorant of the stories' background, is at liberty to laugh inculpably within the circles of rustics into which the narrator leads him. These circles can be as immediate as a film dialogue in close-up: "Talkin about Lester . . . You all talk about him. I got supper waitin on me at the house" (81). Were the oral testimonies positioned after part 3, the novel would read as scandalous as a work by Erskine Caldwell. The reader would find it hard to sympathize with Lester and could not feel amused. Thus the very fact that the oral testimonies are chronologically displaced indicates that the narrative intention is to sell the narrator's empathy for Lester to the reader. What other motive could have moved the narrator to address the reader and propose that Lester, a psycho killer, is a "child of God much like yourself perhaps" (4)? To suspect that McCarthy may have intended to implicate the reader not in the text's empathy with Lester but in some kind of solidarity with his very crimes is completely unwarranted by textual evidence and would constitute a misreading of the overall composition.[16] Closer to the point is Jarrett's observation that the novel's title seems like an "appeal to the democratic egalitarianism at the center of American political rhetoric and to the equally commonplace Christian doctrine of the fundamental equality of all souls" (36). The text strives to build up neither a protagonist representing general moral turpitude nor a demented, freakish outsider, but a sentient human being, ethically derailed and socially estranged, to be sure, but not unaccountable for his actions.

Neither does the text allow for a classification of Lester as a scapegoat of the violent collective that first makes him into what he is, then ostracizes him.[17] While his destruction might seem like a purification of the community he comes from and preys on, and while Lester may well be considered something of a "pariah" (Schafer 117), he is at most a liminal figure, never willfully excluded, "never indicted for any crime" (193). Actually, he is readily incorporated into a background of misfits past and present, such as the hermit (168), Trantham (36), or Reubel (the dump keeper), and notorious troublemakers like Lester's own kin (80–81). Not only do the tall tales testify to his integration but the narrative voice itself also verifies the point in one of the rare direct addresses to the reader: "He could not swim, but how would you drown him? His wrath seemed to buoy him up. Some halt in the way of things seems to work here. See him. You could say that he's sustained by his fellow men, like you" (156). Here, the speaker is not vying for sympathy but berating a collective, that includes the reader, for applying erratic, or bigoted, standards; for confusing moral outrage with sensationalism. Nonetheless, the narrator makes a strong case for the integration of Lester. The story has progressed too far for direct appeals to the reader's empathy, and so the narrator's plea seeks only to assign Lester his rightful place as a freak[18] who has become an intolerable liability for the community.

The vigilante action to which Lester is later subjected brings no ritual purification. No rancor, righteousness, or even hurry enters into the manhunt for Lester. In fact, it is conducted more as if his rampage presented an emergency dire enough to warrant collective action. The endemic violence infesting the hinterland society of *Child of God* is not foregrounded but related in an often roundabout way and it persists unabated and un-atoned throughout. "I never knew such a place for meanness," (164) says a woman in Sevierville. Lester is not altogether wrong when he accuses the sheriff of having "henhouse ways" (56); his taunt is validated by certain episodes, such as that involving the parked couple (44–45).

Communal empathy for Lester might have deeper roots than just a tacit sanctioning of his rampage out of a shared disposition for violence. Empathy for him might even be found on the side of the reader, because at least initially, Grammer argues, Lester "is claiming a role for himself in one of the central dramas in the pastoral republican mythology": "An armed man, prepared to defend the country and his own liberty and property, was for our ancestors the ideal republican citizen, the foundation of stable order: an idea which will seem most familiar to us, perhaps, as it is enshrined in the Second Amendment to the Constitution" (39). Lester's reaction to the age-old trauma of pastoral dispossession may be extreme and perverted, but the trauma itself feels real and worthy of empathy. Hence, to interpret his role as merely that of a pariah and scapegoat seems less than plausible. The novel's ending represents not an exorcism but an epiphanic moment of Lester's coming home. Recanting his life as a criminal and fugitive, he turns himself in as soon as he has dug his way out of the labyrinth of the cave. As he resurfaces he experiences, in succession, an almost sentimental scene of pastoral tranquillity ("beyond the cow was a barn and beyond that a house," 190), a troublesome if healing encounter with an alter ego ("the boy looked like himself," 191), and the dawning of a new day ("roosters were calling," 191). He himself is curiously altered when he presents himself at the hospital reception (192). In short, he is removed from the extreme margin of society that he has occupied, and this not toward the outside, into death or exile, but toward the inside.

The strange form this reintegration takes is his institutionalization and the postmortem. Yet this minimal redemption is anything but incidental or ironic. Lester's body is used for scientific procedures that are detailed as barbaric but are societally sanctioned, "the exploiter of corpses becoming an exploited corpse" (Winchell 305). The function of this turn of events is to confirm that the entire collective is informed by violence of varying degrees. It serves to address the patent ambiguity of "normality" in the context of a latent systemic violence.[19] In this context, even narrative inserts such as hunting tableaux and stories of violent carnival acts are carefully calculated to create a mental and moral setting not only resigned to, but sanctioning, the use of violence as a culturally established mode of conflict resolution on all levels, inside the human community and out. "Lester has become a part of the mythology of his region and has thereby achieved, ironically, a place in the community that has eluded him otherwise. Moreover, since the narration has been so scrupulously decentralized from the beginning, it seems intended to be as much about the place and the people in it as about Lester himself. By these two means Lester becomes something like the spirit of the place, a bizarre aberration certainly, but not so totally dissociated from the people of that place that he doesn't seem somehow like their collective nightmare" (Bell, *Achievement* 54).

At least as important as Lester's identification with the collective are the limits of his deteriorating identification with his personal and the collective self. Certain instances—such as the mention of his "old shed self" (158)—hint at the progressive erosion of the boundaries of Lester's identity. Thus, the motif of the double—familiar in McCarthy's oeuvre—enters the story in the form of Lester's necrophilia and the voided identities of the dead that he remakes in his own image.

Lester's first usurpation of another self is suggested when he takes over where the asphyxiated lover on Frog Mountain left off, assuming the dead man's sexual identity. The narrative perspective (which coincides with Lester's) presents the dead as if they were alive, "just the three of them. He knelt in the seat and leaned over the back and studied the other two" (87). The grotesque narrative reanimation of the dead couple in the car escalates when the reader is told that "the dead man's penis, sheathed in a wet yellow condom, was pointing at him rigidly" and that "[t]he dead man was watching him from the floor of the car" (88).[20] As he merges his identity with those of his dead victims, and as the girls thus become his compound double, he risks the loss of self and sanity in this encounter with his death, because the replication of his finite self implies a sense of continuity that only the death of the self provides. The dissolution of his individuality becomes pathological when he begins to romance dead girls, bestowing upon them the status of living, willing lovers:

> He poured into that waxen ear everything he'd ever thought of saying to a woman. Who could say she did not hear him? (88–89)
>
> He undressed her very slowly, talking to her. [. . .] You been wantin it, he told her. (103)

The more necrophilia takes the place of social interaction, the vaguer becomes his sense of self, until it merges with the dead women's projected identities, open to limitless identification. His fickle gender identity disintegrates completely when he starts cross-dressing: "He'd long been wearing the underclothes of his female victims but now he took to appearing in their outerwear as well. A gothic doll in illfit clothes, its carmine mouth floating detached and bright in the white landscape" (140). The crumbling of Lester's subjectivity is reflected by the narrative perspective when it refers to him as "a small thing" (154), and uses the neutral pronoun "it" to refer to "this thing" during his attack on Greer: "the man looked at whatever it was standing there cursing to itself while it worked the lever of the rifle, an apparition created whole out of nothing" (172–73).[21] Elsewhere, his insanity is made explicit by authorial comment: "He had not stopped cursing. Whatever voice spoke him was no demon but some old shed self that came yet from time to time in the name of sanity, a hand to gentle him back from the rim of his disastrous wrath" (158). Moments such as this one, while illustrating Lester's loss of selfhood, reflect a certain degree of self-awareness. Nonetheless, the passage uses rhetoric too sophisticated to be Lester's and is therefore projected by the narrator. The following two quotes do not seem directly prescribed by the narrative voice (though of course they are, as the rhetoric clarifies) but are made to seem rooted in the protagonist's awareness. Here, Lester's crimes seem remote, no more than a narrative device designed to substantiate a third-person confession, to authenticate his exile, and to situate him as hermit, mystic, and ascetic.

> Ballard lying on his pallet by the fire one evening saw them [bats] come from the dark of the tunnel and ascend through the hole overhead fluttering wildly in the ash and smoke like souls rising from hades. When they were gone he watched the hordes of cold stars sprawled across the smokehole and wondered what stuff they were made of, or himself. (141)
>
> He watched the diminutive progress of all things in the valley, the gray fields coming up black and corded under the plow, the slow green occlusion that the trees were spreading. Squatting there he let his head drop between his knees and he began to cry. (170)

In and of itself, it is not incongruous for Lester to mourn his exclusion from the pastoral dream or from pondering the heavenly bodies before going to sleep. In fact, therein lies his "child of god" simplicity: A more sophisticated observer would know of what stuff stars, if not himself, were made. But the philosophical touch at the end of the first quote and the elegiac verbiage of the second articulates an adjacent, meta-narrative sense of abjection that grounds the novel's pastoralism. Lester's self-abjection, then, is constructed to include the greater abjection of an imaginary pastoral self. Tellingly, Lester's attack on Greer is preceded by a dream image that suggests both his own and the narrator's abjection: "He had resolved himself to ride on for he could not turn back and the world that day was as lovely as any day that ever was and he was riding to his death" (170).[22] Aside from the language, the immediate context further confirms the assumption that the dream reflects the narrator's mood because the preceding sentence divides into two sub-clauses. The second of these represents not Lester's but the narrator's thought without identifying the shift of perspective. Instead of "the only sound he heard" (which would make the observation Lester's) the sentence reads "the only sound was," as if the entire thought was in fact the narrator's. The parenthesis "a lonely piper," being as it were a comment, marks the shift: "Lying awake in the dark of the cave he thought he heard a whistling as he used to when he was a boy in his bed in the dark and he'd hear his father on the road coming home whistling, a lonely piper, but the only sound was the stream where it ran down through the cavern to empty it may be in unknown seas at the center of the earth" (170). Failing to distinguish in any way between the narrator's pensiveness and Lester's, this passage aligns the self-destructive energy of the subsequent dream with that of the narrative consciousness.

In this sense, Lester's self-destruction is an inherent part of the text, independent of any suicidal tendency that one might diagnose for Lester as a person. The key to the interconnection between protagonist and narrator is given in the novel's last part, beginning with Lester's attack on Greer. In its irrationality the attack itself should read like a suicide attempt and form the logical consummation of his self-destructive lifestyle and of the story as well. Why then would the suicidal impulse of this killer's psyche remain unconsummated at this point? Why does the story continue? After the attempt on Greer's life, nothing would seem to remain to be told except his death. Yet narration of his death is deferred for the purpose of inserting another series of episodes. These are as strange as they are essential because they contain the death of his old self and the coming to terms with wilderness.

The episodes in question—narrating Lester's abduction by the vigilantes, his escape into the caves, his odyssey underground, and his eventual self-rescue and return to the hospital—clearly translate the episode into a rebirthing experience because Lester is hardly himself on the remaining pages. Aside from taking a redemptive turn, the concluding chapters stylize his self-liberation from the caves into the recovery of an alternative self. But first things first: The Lester who manages to dig his way out is a changed man in a changed landscape. He emerges from the ground not as a wild man returning into wilderness, but as a penitent who, on his way to the hospital, rediscovers his lost innocence in the double of a boy aboard the bus passing him: "He was trying to fix in his mind where he'd seen the boy when it came to him that the boy looked like himself. This gave him the fidgets and though he tried to shake the image of the face in the glass it would not go" (191). Although he knows that the existence gained by turning himself in will be a marginalized one at best (locked up in a mental institution), his regained sanity ("he had nothing to say to a crazy man" [193]) compels him to submit to societal judgment in return for a restored sense of self: "I'm supposed to be here, he said" (192). As Marx's elaboration of the final episode of the pastoral genre suggests, his decision complies with the typology of the pastoral hero, if in an unconventional way, because "To keep going in the direction of unmodified nature, the hero senses, is to risk another, more dire loss of selfhood" ("Pastoralism" 57). It is precisely the loss of selfhood in the episodes just recounted that provides the key to the alternative pastoral selfhood that is allegorically inscribed into the protagonist.

Allegorical discourse works like a palimpsest, substituting one figure or image for another figure or image of identical meaning, and thus recreating a literary type whose meaning is specific and non-negotiable. Among other things, a literary type would be defined by the "unreflective and unironic action" characterizing Lester's behavior (Bell, "Nihilism" 34), or by having "no capacity of mind or consciousness" (Donoghue 5). In the episode of Lester's return, the meaning that is allegorically conferred upon Lester reconnects to Christian typology (common enough in Southern fiction): It stylizes Lester into a grotesque Christ figure. While the cave odyssey represents a womb- and rebirth-parable, it simultaneously allegorizes the resurrection of Christ in its sequence of interment, underground journey through the valley of death ("a long room filled with bones," 188), resurrection on a Sunday[23] after "three days" (187), and redemption ("He was never indicted for any crime," 193). A redemptive note links the penitent Lester to the figures of Saint Peter and the prodigal son. It points moreover to this act of typological codification itself by extending its implication diachronically through time and synchronically through space: "As he neared the town the roosters were calling. Perhaps they sensed a relief in the obscurity of night that the traveler could not read, though he kept watch eastward. Perhaps some freshness in the air. Everywhere across the sleeping land they called and answered each to each. As in olden times so now. As in other countries here" (191). Lester also reconnects to the figure of Ishmael, sole survivor of another quest and a messenger of bad tidings. Ishmael, in turn, has his own typological precursor, as Marx argues: "The significance that Melville attaches to Ishmael's survival is indicated by the line from Job he takes as the motto of the epilogue: "And I only am escaped alone to tell thee." In other words, Ishmael's relation to us, the readers of *Moby Dick,* is like that of Job's messenger to Job. The calamity he recounts is a portent of further trials to come (*Machine* 287). Lester's return into the community of men serves the same end: To have him embark on a catastrophic quest for a wilderness version of a pastoral self and live to tell the tale.

While the use of allegory here and in the cave episode does nothing to authenticate the story of Lester Ballard, it goes a long way in stylizing the protagonist into a wilderness adaptation of the pastoral hero. It explains the allegorical function that Lester's perverted sexuality serves for the larger context of the meta-narrative. The episode itself contains instances that suggest both the meta-narrative context and Lester's significance for it: "He heard the mice scurry in the dark. Perhaps they'd nest in his skull, spawn their tiny bald and mewling whelps in the lobed caverns where his brains had been. His bones polished clean as eggshells, centipedes sleeping in their marrowed flutes, his ribs curling slender and whitely like a bone flower in the dark stone bowl" (189). This almost baroque *memento mori* image evokes, aside from the mortality of man, a continuity between the protagonist and the cosmos, and this in regard to both its animate and inanimate aspects. While this meditation reads like the protagonist's own astounding insight it refers to a variation of the pastoral hero.

As the narrative progresses apace with Lester's incremental retreat into wilderness and psychosis, Lester's unreflective point of view grounds itself increasingly in a deeper, broader vision. Read superficially, the narrator's empathy with the protagonist's situation may have prompted him to stylize him into a symbol of pastoral, social, or sexual frustration. However, scrutiny of scenes in sequence—such as the final cave episodes—suggests inversely that the narrative situations are carefully composed to articulate issues attendant on Lester's perspective but outside his perceptual horizon. Lester is structurally and semantically situated to channel an eco-pastoral discourse. While it is appropriate to read McCarthy's account of Lester's sexual murders and necrophilia as a diagnosis of his personal sexuality, it is essential to see that this, his psychograph, is couched in a larger reiteration of his story in the form of a narrative quest for continuity with nature that informs any pastoral vision. His maniacal sexuality and the pastoralism of *Child of God* are invested with exactly the same melancholia over an unattainable harmony.

Having understood this, it is all the more surprising that Lester's direct interaction with nature is not conciliatory, but confrontational. The most conspicuous examples are provided whenever Lester issues commands to elements of nature that are not subject to human control, but that nonetheless comply:

> Now freeze, you son of a bitch, he told the night beyond the windowpane. It did. (103)
>
> Die, goddamn you, he said. She did. (119)
>
> He told the snow to fall faster and it did. (139)

These instances seem to contradict the previous assessment of the protagonist's harmony with his environment. One would expect the hero of a wilderness pastoralism to anticipate the egalitarianism of McCarthy's Border Trilogy, in which man takes his place within nature according to a radically democratic cosmology. Instead, *Child of God* offers a pastoral figure who is as wild and as antagonistic as the wild hinterland he roams, kin to the desperadoes in *Blood Meridian*. His attitude toward all living things is grounded in a sensibility reduced to the predatory instinct, his dualism being that of hunter and prey. While incongruent at first glance, what could ultimately be more logical in wilderness pastoralism?

Accordingly, the motif of the hunt runs through the text like a red thread (as it does in *The Orchard Keeper*), stylizing not just Lester into a hunter by ability and inclination, but Sheriff Fate and his posse as well. Lester hardly ever goes unarmed, "the rifle hanging in his hand as if it were a thing he could not get shut of" (41): "He had that rifle from when he was just almost a boy" (57). He levels it at a songbird (25), a cat (26), fish (33), Greer (109), and the auctioneer (7) in quixotic display of his power but without actually firing. He does fire at and kill frogs (33), cattle (34), squirrels (85), and finally people. His marksmanship at the fun fair functions as a singular display of his prowess. He holds the rifle as he talks to the lady in the woods who later charges him with rape; he brings it over to Reubel's, supposedly to hunt rats. He hunts indiscriminately, and hunting comes naturally to him even as he turns to human prey. He stalks Greer from behind as he would an animal, and levels his rifle at Greer "as hunters do" (172). Even the abandoned cabin he inhabits for a while is one frequented by hunters (16) and hounds (23–24).

The boar hunt episode, an allegory of lyrical beauty and thematic prominence, implicates Lester, the remote watcher, "in its holograph of battle" (69). But it also represents a central parable on the changing fortunes of the hunt. The boar, itself a predator, has become the subject of a hunt; one of the bloodhounds, the boar's hunter, is killed in turn. The huntsmen following in the rear eventually kill the boar but are themselves observed by a hunter of humans, Lester. Finally, the closing of the episode introduces the ultimate hunter, death itself, as "the fading light" (69). The whole twilight tableau is suffused with a plaintive air, as if hinting at the finitude of all things. The hunters are reduced to animate subjects among others, predators among other predators. One hundred pages later, the negative egalitarianism of a similar scene is articulated more clearly for the same watcher, Lester: "In the spring Ballard watched two hawks couple and drop, their wings upswept, soundless out of the sun to break and flare above the trees and ring up again with thin calls. He eyed them on, watching to see if one were hurt. He did not know how hawks mated but he knew that all things fought" (169). Shortly before Lester's apprehension as a hunted criminal, the scene reveals his predatory rationale. It illustrates the fact that for him sexuality represents but another aspect of the struggle for survival, a reversible struggle between hunter and hunted. Lester has fully succumbed to the predatory instincts he finds in himself and in the wilderness around him. In this scene, and in this scene only, he seems to be in harmony with what Bell calls "the ecological coherence of his environment" (*Achievement* 64).

What his construction as an ignoble savage outside any conceivable human ethos, "a protohuman simian creature, an ape, a caveman" (Bartlett 13), creates is the perspective of a deranged consciousness. The extremely marginalized angle that Lester provides would not otherwise be attainable. The pastoral protagonist is defined by Marx as "an efficacious mediator between the realm of organized society and the realm of nature." He is an "ascetic . . . independent, self-sufficient and, like the rugged western hero of American mythology, singularly endowed with the qualities needed to endure long periods of solitude, discomfort, and deprivation" ("Pastoralism" 43). Elsewhere Marx writes: "The difference between the typical American hero and the shepherd in traditional versions of pastoral is suggested by Renato Poggioli's account of that archetypal figure as one who 'lives a sedentary life even in the open, since he prefers to linger in a grove's shade rather than to wander in the woods. He never confronts the true wild, and this is why he never becomes even a part-time hunter.' Given the circumstances of American life, our heroes do confront the true wild, and they often become hunters. But it is striking to notice how often they are impelled to restrict or even renounce their hunting" (*Machine* 246). This certainly applies to Lester, if in a way that makes him a sinister parody of the American pastoral hero: Instead of asceticism, one finds squalor; instead of independence, deracination; instead of self-sufficiency, improvisation; instead of rugged resourcefulness, primitivism. Bell's assessment that Lester represents "the negative image of Arthur Ownby in *The Orchard Keeper* in this respect, not at home or at ease anywhere" (*Achievement* 64) is correct, but it is qualified by the fact that the wild nature in *Child of God* is simply not a place to come home to.

To sum up: If wilderness, that is, the part of nature untouched by human cultivation, were to enter into the aesthetic discourse of pastoral writing, it could only imply an anthropomorphous projection onto wilderness, unless a representational mode could be defined that matched the non-humanized nature of wilderness by being as little humanized, stylized, and romanticized as possible. Such a discourse would have to revert to the near-zero level of a primitive mind (whose engagement with his surroundings would run the risk of remaining culturally undecipherable), or the mind of a madman like Lester, who combines a primitive state of mind with intelligible, if psychopathic, articulation. The answer to the question why *Child of God* presents wilderness beauty and pastoral melancholia side by side with extreme depravity is that the protagonist's depravity marks the premise for representing wilderness beauty in its true, feral state. His unique psychology makes it discursively possible to describe the liminal point between Man and Not-Man with virtually no reflection. The narrator's compassion for his protagonist reduces itself to an aesthetic infatuation with a privileged narrative vehicle for the wilderness turn in McCarthy's pastoralism.

What this wilderness perspective can do for pastoral writing becomes apparent when it combines with the melancholy style already discussed in the context of *The Orchard Keeper,* specifically its paratactic effect: As it levels the narrative structure (grammatically), likens one incident or aspect to another (metaphorically), and puts the present in sequence with past and future (allegorically), the semantic effect of this wilderness-minded discourse is equalization on all levels. Carrying over into the pastoral differentiation between urban, middle, and wild spaces, it erases—through its emphasis on survival—the distinction between pastoral beauty and wilderness beauty, between wildness within and wilderness without, between the community of men and the community of nature. Textual evidence of this egalitarian discourse can be found everywhere in *Child of God* (emphases added to identify the relevant phrases):

> Given charge Ballard would have made things more orderly *in the woods and in men's souls.* (136; equating wild nature with mankind)
>
> . . . he watched the hordes of cold stars sprawled across the smokehole and he wondered what stuff *they were made of, or himself.* (141; equating the materiality of the individual subject with that of the cosmos)

Voiding the notion of human harmony with nature of its traditional hierarchy, passages such as these infuse all things, natural and manmade, with a shared materiality.

Ultimately, all figures of the novel are shown to contain the wildness, the indifference and the silence of nature within themselves.[24] Yet, differences in degree of wildness prevail, as if to show that a wilderness consciousness is unsustainable without the loss of a human sense of self. What brings about the failure of the narrative wilderness quest in *Child of God* is the absolute indifference of nature toward such a consciousness. The narrative sacrifices everything human about its protagonist and gains nothing except a fleeting insight. Indeed it seems as if the terrifying indifference of nature vis-à-vis humanity sounded the final note of this tour de force: "In the evening a jeep descended the log road towing a trailer in the bed of which lay seven bodies bound in muslin like enormous hams. As they went down the valley in the new fell dark basking nighthawks rose from the dust in the road before them with wild wings and eyes red as jewels in the headlights" (196–97). This, like all of McCarthy's novels, centers in the tension between wilderness as an ideal and as a source of horror. This novel's achievement is to divest pastoralism of its moral middle ground to redefine pastoralism according to a wilderness aesthetic all its own.

Outer Dark (1968)

McCarthy's second novel is structured as a purely allegorical composition rather than a mimetic work of fiction. Critics have acknowledged that the novel's "world is an allegory" (Davenport 4), that "the timelessness of the story gives it a blurred Kafkaesque quality, verging on allegory" (Schafer 111), and that "the dreamlike setting and pace bring an almost medieval aura of allegory to the events" (Bell, *Achievement* 33). The allegorical nature of the triune (the three marauders) is also implied in epithets like "figures of *time*" and death (Grammer 35), "avenging angels" and "crazed furies" (Schafer 111), or "a mad variation on the Magi" (Leiter 91). In fact, the novel is devoid of any sign of realism, except for the *sur*-realism of gothic fiction. The use of gothic imagery and allegory in the novel positions *Outer Dark* within the tradition of Southern gothic fiction, while pastoral nostalgia culminates in absolute melancholia and in this sense propels traditional pastoralism to its worst, if logical, conclusion.

Generically, *Outer Dark* represents a gothic more than a pastoral novel even though its Southern setting is marked by a rusticity bordering on the primitive. The novel's plot is as simple as it is strange: Rinthy Holme has given birth to the child of her brother Culla, who abandons the child in the forest but is found out by Rinthy. The baby is abducted by a tinker, and the bulk of the story covers the journeys of Rinthy (seeking to recover her child) and

Culla (searching for Rinthy). They never meet again. A third journey motif covers the crime spree of the triune who cuts a swath of death in the wake of the siblings' progress, and who eventually takes the child from the tinker, then murders it in Culla's presence. Much remains to be said as Culla's road terminates in a swamp, Rinthy's in the glade where child and tinker died. The paucity of plot structure, the absence of verifiable references to time and place, and the unmitigated horror render the novel as fantastic as the fairy tale of Hansel and Gretel, and Sullivan says as much: "So we move through a world of curiously contrived ferries, fat men who live in decaying houses, preachers who attempt to inspire bloodshed, criminals who kill for the joy of killing. The question is not whether these things taken separately exist, but rather what kind of world they come together to create, what kind of unity they make. And the answer is: none; they remain separate features of the surrealist landscape" ("Flowers" 661). While Faulkner's use of grotesque or gothic elements fails to diminish the realism of settings, scenes and figures, *Outer Dark* rarely provides names, let alone satisfying profiles. The characters are grotesque in the manner of solitary gargoyles, woven into the text not so much as individuals in their own right but rather as typological variations on gothic archetypes.

In keeping with the gothic tradition, the novel manifests a gnostic polarity of good versus evil. Gnosticism, understood as "the belief that knowledge available to men (gnosis) can be used to change the very constitution of being" (Simpson, *Garden* 76), amounts in the context of the Southern pastoral to an ill-fated escapism that ideally would isolate a pastoral community from the corruptions of urban civilization. Instead, it boils down to "a denial of history which becomes, at last, a denial of being; a desire to remake man and his world according to utopian theory" (Grammer 31). The preoccupation of Southern gothicism has thus been to capture the pastoral break when evil reenters the utopian pastoral community, that is, "the moment when a community organized as a refuge from history is forced to confront it" (Grammer 35). Yet the evil irrupting from within the pastoral world of *Outer Dark* mocks the very distinction between good and evil, between outside intrusion and civic strife. The sense of evil remains vague and endemic.

Among the constants of gothicism that Kerr lists are "psychological interest and concern with the irrational and the unconscious, the dream side of the psyche; appalling situations; a

Calvinistic Manichean polarity of good and evil and/or ambivalence in the moral attitudes of the characters; the abandonment of realism as a major aim; the use of setting and atmosphere to create a mood" (6). Grotesque imagery functions as one of the principal devices to cause a "realistic displacement which conceals Gothic structures" (Kerr 28), and grotesque aspects inform characters and setting everywhere in *Outer Dark*, such as the tinker ("a small gnomic creature wreathed in a morass of grizzled hair," 6), the supplicants ("A delegation of human ruin," 5), the noseless crone ("long bat's nostrils," 57), the hermitic crone ("the stooped and hooded anthropoid," 108), the hog drovers ("all hairyfaced and filthy and half toothless," 220), and the infant at the center of the story (e.g., 231). The novel's grotesque aesthetic in itself discourages a realistic reading. Kerr (picking up an idea by Alfred Appel) links the grotesque in gothic fiction to "the breakdown of order into dream effects" (20): "The grotesque is characterized by a distortion of the external world, by the description of human beings in nonhuman terms, and by the displacement we associate with dreams. The infinite possibilities of the dream inform the grotesque at every turn, suspending the laws of proportion and symmetry: our deepest promptings are projected into the details of the scene—inscape as landscape" (21). This is important to bear in mind because some of the characters in *Outer Dark* seem to have been directly evoked by Culla's dream of the opening pages of the novel: the "parson or what looked like one" (221), the hog drovers, the blind preacher near the end who virtually retells that dream as if he had witnessed it. Foremost among the grotesques who resemble residual dream figures is the nameless child, whom Culla "would have taken . . . for some boneless cognate of his heart's dread had the child not cried" (18). Introduced as "the nameless weight in her belly" (5), the child in fact personifies the guilt that Culla feels over the incest. More obviously, the triune's "consubstantial monstrosity" (129) seems like the projection of a schizophrenic mind.

Upon closer scrutiny, the surrealist quality in *Outer Dark* presents itself wherever the narrative flow is invaded by imagery fusing the immaterial (such as dream consciousness) with the material (such as setting). Evidence of a surrealist transfer of dream images to the plot level is given by numerous comparisons of scenery to dreamscape. Culla sees the people in Well's Station move "beneath the blinding heat like toilers in a dream" (134), he sees hanged men appear in the first light of day "alien and unreal like figures from a dream" (146), the "minktrapper materialized for him out of the glare of the sun like some trembling penitent" (125); and shoats run past him "like creatures in a dream" (219). The tinker "started in his traces like one wrenched from a trance" (184), and Rinthy "rose half tranced from the bed" because perhaps "some dream had moved her so" (211). Most notably, however, the triune is "endowed with a dream's redundancy" (231).

Kerr proposes "a direct relationship between Gothicism and surrealism" and defines surrealism as "the belief in the superior reality of certain forms of association theretofore neglected, in the omnipotence of dream, and in the disinterested play of thought" (12). In *Outer Dark* surrealist narration manifests itself in compositional incongruence. Incongruent figures, reminiscent of Culla's dream, include the beehiver, the false reverend, and the blind preacher; semantic incongruence occurs when Culla hears "no sound save a faint moaning like the wind but there was no wind" (231), when the leader remarks about his henchman "[h]e's close, but I keep at it" (178), and when Rinthy watches "a huge horse emerging seared and whole from the sun's eye" (212), and in the form of attributes such as "poisoned grass" (229). Most likely, these surreal moments serve to project evil (the story's principal concern) out of their psychical realm and into the narrative landscape. Bell writes that "like a curse that he [Culla] has brought upon the world, he now has remade the world in his own blighted image," and that "eventually, there is hardly any significant difference, ontologically, between his dream life and the real world" (*Achievement* 39). The insertion of surrealist imagery turns the representation of landscape in much of *Outer Dark* into an obvious representation of the inscape of Culla's psyche.

Hence, the surrealist aspects in *Outer Dark* translate inner ruin into the ruinous aspects of a gothic landscape. Among the negatively picturesque images are the descriptions of the crone's house, which "was grown with a rich velour of moss and lichen and brooded in a palpable miasma of rot" (109); the snake hunter's house, in which "On the lower walls grew scalloped shelves of fungus and over the untrod parts of the floor lay a graygreen mold like rotting fur" (121–22); and the deserted cabin in which Culla "could see nothing plane or plumb anywhere" (195). Images of ruins and decay commonly reflect pastoral nostalgia in Southern literature, yet in *Outer Dark* pastoral decay escalates into universal desolation. In fact, the surrealist adaptation of Southern stock images seems to create a virtual Southern microcosm.

Moreover, *Outer Dark* does not merely incorporate allegorical elements but is structured as a pastoral parable from cover to cover. Davenport's notion that "McCarthy is unashamedly an allegorist" (4) is borne out, for instance, when Culla's guilt causes him to invest the forest with punitive powers: "the trees beginning to close him in, malign and baleful shapes that reared like enormous androids provoked at the alien insubstantiality of this flesh colliding among them" (17). Other examples of pathetic fallacies in the text include "naked trees in attitudes of agony" (242) or "Dark birds . . . crossing the fields to the west like heralds of some coming dread" (188). Matter becomes animate, as a boot "sank instantly as if a hand in the river had claimed it" (166), as rapids sound "like the stammering of the cloistered mad" (167), as "the squatting shape of the windowsash came and went on the wood floor like something breathing" (150), as Culla's "shadow moiled cant and baneful over the lot" (91), or as the sun "buckled and dark fell like a shout" (5). Even man-made articles betray a sinister agency, such as when "the upper windows watched them with wrinkled sunstricken glass" (83). Inversely, Rinthy surrenders her human agency when following the tinker's "lonely tolling tinware like some creature rapt and besorced by witches' music, demon piping" (187). The effect is the creation of a fairy-tale world.

The microscopic quality of this setting becomes apparent first of all because the text omits any exposition of the location. Bell writes, "The two principal characters of *Outer Dark* wander about as if in a maze that has no center to it or exit" (*Achievement* 34). Grammer comments on "the vagueness of its temporal setting: sometime before the advent of the internal combustion engine, one gathers; beyond that it is difficult to say" (34). Sullivan makes a similar observation, but draws no structural inference: "Time and place remain undefined. From the language we know we are in the South, from the trappings of life we know we are in the past; but where in the South, how far into the past, we have no way of telling" ("Flowers" 662). Together, these observations serve to confirm a single point: The fact that the world of *Outer Dark* exists in an unspecified time indicates nothing so much as allegorical structure, since "allegory exists entirely within an ideal time that is never here and now but always a past or an endless future" (de Man 220). Fletcher argues that the "apocalyptic escape into infinite space and time" (23) typical of allegorical writing is motivated less by a fascination with a mechanistic cosmos than by the desire to negotiate major social and spiritual concerns from the narrative distance that such a projected cosmos affords.

The spiritual concern underlying *Outer Dark,* enacted in a sinister parable on the Southern pastoral, is clearly the aspect of evil in Southern pastoralism as such. When he writes that McCarthy's "responsibility as a storyteller includes believing with his characters in the devil, or at least in the absolute destructiveness of evil" (4), Davenport actually suggests that the entire setting is allegorized as a pastoral world cursed by evil. The evil that suffuses setting and plot action is opposed solely by the counter discourse of the text itself, and in this sense the novel lacks epiphanies of absolute good, even in Rinthy's state of grace.[25] As usual, the evil plaguing the pastoral world does not intrude from without, but originates inside the pastoral world. What is unexpected is its being caused by the universal awareness of evil more than by evil action: It is the imagination of evil that precipitates violence.

Benjamin's observation that "knowledge, not action, is the most immanent mode for the existence of evil" (*Trauerspiel* 205) refers to baroque allegory, yet the idea that mental complicity with evil may provide the key to the novel's sense of evil obviously applies to Culla because of the novel's allegorical nature. For one thing, Culla is repeatedly blamed for acts of violence that he does not seem to have committed but that he knows about. He is suspected of having desecrated a grave although the text clearly identifies the triune as perpetrator, the leader wearing the dead man's "shapeless and dusty suit of black linen" (95, cf. 88). Dreading another manhunt, Culla makes a getaway from Well's Station where Salter, two mill hands, and Clark, the rash entrepreneur, are murdered. While many of the atrocities are clearly committed by the triune—not Culla—the marauders' itinerary strangely coincides with Culla's. The murders occur either right before he arrives at, or right after he departs from, the respective crime sites. The snake hunter is killed after Culla's visit (129), the ferryman dies in the course of Culla's crossing (165), and the triune's theft of garden implements occurs while Culla is talking to their owner (35, 47). Absurdly, the triune's leader, who appears to be omniscient, counts among those who indict Culla, such as when he twice says "I allowed you was the ferryman" (171) as if to blame Culla for his death; when he asks him, "How come ye to run your sister off?" (178); and when he suspects "you got this thing here in her belly your own self and then laid it off on that tinker" (233).

The knowledge Culla has of the triune's violence, and the triune's knowledge of Culla's situation clearly establish a mutual complicity, and Culla's growing feelings of paranoia insinuate as much. In the hog drovers' scene this is facetiously acknowledged by the diabolic reverend, who is probably none other than the triune's leader: "Tore up with guilt. The preacher nodded sad and negative. Plumb tore up with it" (222). Assuming that this complicity with evil is predicated not on the evil act but on the knowledge of evil, Culla's sins of incest and child abandonment automatically make him a familiar of other, or all, evil in the text: an unwitting avatar of evil. His firsthand knowledge of the atrocities, his refusal to confront and confess his own trespasses, and his criminal indifference vis-à-vis his child's fate constitute the nadir of the intratextual morality. Culla's immoral state is highlighted by his admission "I ain't never prayed" (240), his description as "gracelorn" (241), and his lack of piety when "praying silent and godless in his heart" (167) or "staring in mute prayer" (182).

Culla's complicity with evil comes closest to being formulated during his first encounter with the triune. The leader advises Harmon repeatedly to leave Culla alone, as if he intended to spare him for a specific purpose. His absurd hospitality seems designed to coax Culla into negotiating something like a pact with the devil. Three times the leader seeks to associate him with the ferryman. His remarks to Culla either project his agency in the ferry disaster ("What did ye do with the horse?" 173; "Did that ferryman not have nary better shirt than that?" 176), or they imply an agency Culla could claim if he so desired ("I think maybe you are somebody else," 179; "You may get there [nowhere] yet," 181; "That ain't all, is it?" 181). When Culla denies knowledge of Rinthy's whereabouts with the words "I ain't studied it," the leader openly rejects Culla's claim to be unaware of his complicity with the triune: "Yes, the man said. You've studied it" (182). In the Kafkaesque incongruence of this nocturnal scene, Culla's exemption from the triune's wrath loses its mystery, as he is "finally offered a sinister facsimile of friendship, an insinuated blood brotherhood, by a trio of night riders who phlegmatically murder and pillage, leaving behind them, for Culla to negotiate, an evil, circumambient wake" (Bell, *Achievement* 35). Culla's knowledge of evil becomes the allegorical causation of the violence, and he himself an agent of evil.

If one assumed that the triune is called forth by Culla's sense of guilt, then it would seem logical to say that these supernatural characters—"seeming blind with purpose" (*Outer Dark* 35)—represent allegorical aspects of Culla's own self that he projects into the allegorical landscape. Since the theme of terrorism is associable with the character of Culla, but is not restricted to his point of view because terrorist violence is endemic to the textual whole, it is safe to draw the following conclusion: If the novel's allegoresis conditions the narrator's perception of not just Culla but of other characters and of nature as well, then this uniform mode of characterization qualifies these other characters as allegorical figures. What is more, if the allegorical theme implicates the protagonist more than the other figures, and does so in a manner that defines the implication of other figures along the lines of *his* implication, then there is reason to think of Culla as the head of an allegorical compound character, and of applicable other figures as the subcharacters of this compound-character. The following excerpt (again from the campfire scene) illustrates the concept because it shows how Culla's foreshortened vision actually *creates* an image of Satan. It ties the narrative vision of evil to *his* paranoid perspective: "Holme looked at the man. The fire had died some and he could *see him better,* sitting beyond it and *the scene compressed* into a kind of *depthlessness* so that the black woods beyond them *hung across his eyes oppressively* and the man *seemed* to be seated in the fire itself, cradling the flames to his body *as if* there was something there beyond all warming" (179; emphases added). Like Benjy in *The Sound and the Fury,* according to whose mongoloid vision the golf flag "flapped *on* the bright grass and the trees" (3; emphasis added), not *above* the grass and *before* the trees, Culla affects a two-dimensional and strongly biased cognition. Projecting the fiery aspect of the leader (and so being able to "see him better") Culla visualizes a folkloric picture of the devil: One of the man's boots is "cleft from tongue to toe like a hoof" (176), "his eyes were shadowed lunettes with nothing there at all" (171), the meat he offers "was dusted with ash, tasted of sulphur" (172), and "there was but a single cleft and yellow serpent tongue of flame standing among the coals" (181).[26] Clearly, Culla's projection of everything evil onto this figure defines the leader—who refuses to surrender his name, just like Mephisto in Goethe's *Faust*—as an evil archetype. As such, he is not simply *like* Satan, but one of his avatars.

Strangely, Culla is not just imagining this (the narrator invests him with supernatural abilities), because the leader talks about things he cannot know (for example, that the boots are stolen, or that there was a rider on the ferry) or speaks as if he caused them to be (claiming to have waited for Culla "all day and half the night" [178]). For Culla and the narrator, though not for other figures in the text, the leader is omniscient and omnipotent, and this is not because Culla misunderstands but because the killers' diabolical aspects are seen from both the narrator's and Culla's points of view. They have no existence outside Culla's mind and the narrative consciousness because the triune remains invisible to everyone but Culla and the narrator, and the former is clearly made to share in the latter's sense of abjection. If the triune in fact represents the incarnation of Culla's guilty despair, there is allegorical truth in comparing the triune to "revenants that reoccur in lands laid waste with fever: spectral, palpable as stone" (231). Originating in Culla's abject self, these sub-characters represent his fantasies of omnipotence and death: "Just like the deeply meaningful allegories, specters are apparitions from the kingdom of sorrow; they are attracted by the mourner, by him who ponders portents and prospects" (Benjamin, *Trauerspiel* 172). Fletcher practically equates the allegorical character with a compound character: "The allegorical hero is not so much a real person as he is a generator of other secondary personalities, which are partial aspects of himself. . . . A systematically complicated character will generate a large number of other protagonists who react against or with him in a syllogistic manner" (35). Arnold inadvertently supports this interpretation when writing: "As in Melville's *The Confidence Man*, a work worth further comparison to this one, the possibility of multiple identities abounds in *Outer Dark*" ("Naming" 53). As Culla, his child, and the mute gang member begin to resemble each other, the masquerade of allegorical correspondences threatens to encompass all major characters. The triune's leader seems to take on the guises of the beehiver, warning Culla about Cheatham (82), the head of the lynch mob (95), and the reverend (221) because he introduces himself elsewhere as a "minister" (129). If Culla perpetuates his picaresque journey, then the tinker lends himself to interpretation as Culla's aged replica. Two generations hence, he might, like the tinker, reflect: "I've not got soul one in this world save a old halfcrazy sister that nobody never would have like they never would me. I been rocked and shot at and whipped and kicked and dogbit from one end of this state to the other" (193). Culla is *already* being ostracized wherever he goes, he *already* has a half crazy sister, and he has a motive for abducting a baby and bringing it to his sister. So the tinker's itinerary arguably represents a fourth variation on the siblings' quests (the triune's travels being the third).

The typological replication of characters matches the replication of plot structures. Plot replication becomes apparent, for instance, when Culla's journey ends in a swamp resembling the swamp where he abandoned the child, and when Rinthy's, Culla's, and the tinker's journeys all lead back to a glade very much like the one occupied by the Holmes' cabin.[27] In this glade, where the itineraries of Culla, Rinthy, the tinker, and the triune intersect, all quests are foreclosed. Rinthy's child is murdered here, as is the tinker; the triune disappears, and for Culla the glade is "a place of judgment" (Arnold, "Naming" 51) where he passes up the chance to redeem his child and himself.[28] Following the novel's denouement the siblings recommence their purgatorial sojourns as in a new turn of the wheel of fortune. The ritualistic pattern of these subplots is complemented by moments of repetitive action within the course of the respective journeys. Each of the nomadic figures keeps reenacting a certain, identical situation: Culla's behavioral pattern is that of taking work and fleeing before finishing, and being paid for, the job; Rinthy's is that of being taken in by hospitable strangers and leaving suddenly; and the triune's is that of befriending their victims in farcical camaraderie before murdering them. These patterns of repetition—striking in their symmetry—represent but modifications of the theme of alienation. They have to be differentiated from the circular plot progression discussed above.

The principal modes of allegorical action in *Outer Dark*, then, are ritual progress (the circular journeys) and symmetry (repetitive situations). Allegorical action serves to repeat a single theme (rather than to further the plot progression), as if to master a given trauma through liturgical reiteration. Fletcher writes that the allegorist "creates a ritual" whose "effect is to allow a degree of certainty in a world of flux. By making lists (naturalism), by creating complicated 'double plots' (pastoral), . . . the allegorist slows and regulates the pace of the existence his fiction represents" (343–44). In analogy to paradigmatic doubling, parataxis further identifies multileveled repetition as the principal structural device used in *Outer Dark*. As discussed in the context of *The Orchard Keeper,* parataxis "implies a structuring of sentences such that they do not convey any distinctions of higher or lower order" (Fletcher 162) since it positions clauses and phrases in symmetrical isolation, either separating them through punctuation or linking them by noncausal conjunctions. In *Outer Dark,* examples of paratactic structuring include the doubling even of single words such as "from dark to dark" (5, 17), "long and long" (17, 211), "wail on wail" (18), "crash on crash" (108), "Far and far" (190), and "stepping softly and soft their voices" (23), to say nothing of the run-on sentences for which McCarthy's prose is known. Like all of McCarthy's novels, *Outer Dark* is characterized by the striking contrast between an opulent iconography and the paratactic sentence structure in which it is couched. So the compositional unity of *Outer Dark* is effected by a ritualized and symmetric organization of picaresque plotlines, an episodic structure, an emblematic iconography, and a paratactic syntax. The coalescence of these components in a convoluted mosaic opens onto the question of theme, the hub of any allegory's compositional unity.

As it superimposes a thematic grid upon the narrative progression, "allegory implies a dominance of theme over action and image" (Fletcher 304), a privileging of dogmatic, nonmimetic representation. Interestingly, the allegorist's panoply of devices—nonmimetic intention, formal repetition, and dominance of theme—is paralleled in the sublimating effort that the melancholy psyche makes to transcend its alienation. "Sublimation's dynamics, by summoning up primary processes and idealization, weaves a *hypersign* around and within the depressive void. This is *allegory,* as lavishness of that which *no longer is,* but which regains for myself a higher meaning because I am able to remake nothingness" (Kristeva, *Sun* 99). The nodal points between allegory and psychoanalysis may be identified by recalling Lacan's words "that the unconscious is structured in the most radical way like a language"

(Lacan 234). In the present context one would have to invert his dictum to say that the allegorical language of *Outer Dark* is structured in the most radical way like the unconscious of the melancholy narrator. The description of symbolic action in allegorical and psychoanalytical discourse runs along parallel lines. And the languages of both allegory and dream imagery are marked by the use of theme, and by secondary meaning, surrealist paradoxes, and ambiguous character profiles. Both allegory and psychoanalysis are preoccupied with signifying the non-signifiable (such as loss or death).

The prevailing themes in *Outer Dark* encode loss in one form or another: silence, blindness, muteness, destruction, and ultimately death. Bell concedes that Culla's world "is a vacancy and a silence, and his wordless wandering is only an extension of it in another form. Dreamlike and oppressive, his rural landscape with its blank, unsettled spaces has become the image of an inexplicable emptiness and loss" (*Achievement* 38). Possibly, the novel's allegorical composition serves to inscribe a meta-narrative melancholia. The analogies between the compulsive speech of melancholics and allegory regarding form (repetition) and content (loss) "refer allegory, as a mode of communication, back to some kind of essential behavior, which we find in the skeletal structure of the compulsive ritual" (Fletcher 302). Allegory and melancholia mutually complement each other. Both are concerned with what is absent, lost, or part of the past, "the meaning constituted by the allegorical sign" being the repetition "of a previous sign with which it can never coincide, since it is of the essence of this previous sign to be pure anteriority" (de Man 209–10), whereas melancholia is insistent in its grief over a loss that can neither be remembered nor forgotten by the melancholy self. Compulsive repetition marks both allegorical discourse and melancholy psychosis.

Chief indication for a melancholy mood imposed by the narrative consciousness is the implausible alienation and abjection of protagonists Rinthy and Culla. Exceeding even the alienation of Joanna Burden and Joe Christmas in *Light in August* who "are essentially nomads, people on the move" (Bleikasten 314), the alienation of the siblings is absolute and is matched only by that of the tinker. "They ain't a soul in this world but what is a stranger to me," says Rinthy (29); "I ain't got sign one of kin on this earth," says Culla (207); "I've not got soul one in this world save a old halfcrazy sister," says the tinker (192–93)—and these are key sentences of the novel. Bell calls the text a "disturbing, powerful representation of not being at home in the world" (*Achievement* 33). "The whole social atmosphere of *Outer Dark* is one of near-total estrangement," says Grammer (37). Social conventions are constantly broken, relations teeter on the brink of violence, and each encounter is a confrontation marked by phobia and paranoia.

Culla, above all, is subjected to alienation, resembling an outcast "culled" from the community of men, fatherless and "godless" (167). He is also subject to self-abjection, which (according to Lacanian psychoanalysis) in a real-life person would be brought on by the disintegration of the ego under the onslaught of an internalized *alter ego*. Usurping the space of the ego, this *alter ego*, the imaginary Dead Father, "precedes and possesses me, and through such possession causes me to be. A possession previous to my advent" (Kristeva, *Horror* 10). Normally, the aspects of self that are lost with the subject's entry into the symbolic order of language are abjected as the impossible memory of a primal unity, so that "I become a *subject* capable of dealing with *objects* only by virtue of having constituted a domain of the *abject*" (Boothby 65). The abject reemerges if the subject denies itself the negation of the loss and induces an unending pursuit of the lost object, because it has no other identity by which to define its self. Abjection of self is experienced by the subject "when that subject, weary of fruitless attempts to identify with something on the outside, finds the impossible within; when it finds that the impossible constitutes its very *being*, that it *is* none other than abject" (Kristeva, *Horror* 5). Thus, a life in abjection is a forfeited existence lived in exclusion from one's own self.

The loss at issue for Culla is that he leads the existence of a disenfranchised yeoman, unable to conform to the symbolic order of an allegorized Calvinism. His melancholy paranoia is induced by his inability to abide by the internalized code of the Dead Father, namely the role model of Southern yeomanry. The role of the Dead Father can be elucidated with the help of an intertextual comparison of the siblings to Joe and Joanna in *Light in August*. The point is inspired by Bleikasten's argument that "Joe's and Joanna's encounter is the fortuitous but fatal collision of two lives under the same curse, the same paternal *malediction*, and their affair the inevitable working out of two complementary self-destructive designs" (320). As Bleikasten elaborates, "The Father—especially the Dead Father—is always the one who names, separates, places, marks, and casts the spell, whether through his voice or his eyes" (319). Just as Joe and Joanna have internalized the paternal symbolic order to a point that erases their own selves, abjection of self defines the state of Culla's psyche (more so than Rinthy's). In this sense, Culla's inability to fix (30) or sell (56) his late father's rifle—phallic symbol of paternal omnipotence—exemplifies his psychic crisis. Culla's failed identification with an absconding father figure ("He's dead," 207) indicates his internalization of the patriarchal ethos that terrorizes his ego into abjection. The workings of Thanatos are precisely this, the destruction not of the physical body but of the "imaginary form of the body that models the ego" (Boothby 39) by an absolutely powerful Other.

Relevant evidence in *Outer Dark* are all moments informed by guilty, paranoid behavior such as Culla's frantic flight, "careering through the woods with his hands outstretched before him against whatever the dark might hold" (17); his pleading gesture of despair, "bearing his clenched hands above him threatful, supplicant, to the mute and windy heavens" (33); his suspicious behavior in Cheatham, beginning "to shift about uneasily" (88) until he triggers pursuit by a posse; his underdog behavior that causes the squire to prod him "Come on man. What is it you've done" (46); or the pose "like one arraigned" (235) that he assumes before the triune. It would take little for him to establish himself in whatever small position within the rustic world of *Outer Dark,* for it is not his poverty that sets him apart in this squalid country, nor is there a scarcity of jobs. Yet Culla does nothing to improve his station, and yields to inner paralysis ("not listening, never listening," 9).

Read as two avatars of a single subject, Rinthy and Culla represent melancholia in its two principal aspects: abjection and paranoia. Rinthy represents the abjection of loss and thwarted desire in her futile quest for her child and a home, whereas Culla personifies the paranoia in his reiteration of emotions such as guilt, despair, and anxiety. Because non-negated, these emotions surface in visions of mindless violence. Rinthy's and Culla's separate, if synchronous, quests illustrate "that *want* and *aggressivity* are chronologically separable but logically coextensive" (Kristeva, *Horror* 39). Although the chance to reverse their abjection is repeatedly offered to both Rinthy and Culla[29] and is moreover suggested by the eventual disappearance of the triune, the narrator does not intend to resolve the characters' fates but to reiterate them indefinitely in allegoresis of their own pastoral melancholia.

In her discussion of the despondency permeating Dostoyevsky's work, Kristeva names suicide and terrorism as the "two solutions, both fatal, to suffering in Dostoyevsky—the ultimate veil of chaos and destruction" (*Sun* 186). But the terrorism visited upon the pastoral world of *Outer Dark* arguably enacts the melancholy auto-aggression of the narrator in the triune's agency. The fact that Culla's complicity with the triune calls these subcharacters into being does not imply his consent to, or even awareness of, the triune's genesis; no pact is signed. The complicity is inscribed by the narrator who creates the characters, the pastoral world, and the terrorism in the image of his own psyche. *Outer Dark* consequently represents a landscape of the narrative psyche, a "sparse and bitter land" (54) indeed. Since the narrator's pastoral nostalgia seems to have gone berserk to the point that it seeks desolation of the garden rather than acceptance and sublimation of the loss of the pastoral dream, the narrative intention of *Outer Dark* must be to dismember Southern pastoralism as such, and this out of a melancholia so profound that it constructs a sinister parable on the demise of a myth out of the very iconography of the myth itself. The novel in effect refers to a narrative consciousness plagued by the abjection of a literary tradition.

This argument is elucidated by instances of direct intertextuality of *Outer Dark* with antecedent Southern fiction, specifically with *Light in August,* because these suggest McCarthy's continuation of an older pastoralism for the purpose of destroying it. *Light in August* draws on diverse narrative styles to enrich a realistic narrative, whereas *Outer Dark* is structured as a book-length allegory working with pseudo-realistic conceits. But *Light in August*'s Lena Grove, for one, does bear the marks of an allegorical persona because "Lena holds the novel together, enfolds it in her monumental serenity, makes it what it is: a story full of sound and fury set against a background of pastoral stillness, a tale of darkness fringed with light" (Bleikasten 275). Lena moves in the mystic light of August, Rinthy in an "agony of sunlight" (97). Both wear the color of the Madonna—dressed in "a shapeless garment of faded blue" (*Light in August* 9) and "a blue dress" (*Outer Dark* 126), respectively. Lena is twenty (*Light in August* 4–5), Rinthy "nineteen year old" (*Outer Dark* 126). Both are orphaned, both are Ceres figures of pastoral fertility, and yet Rinthy seems to be the very shadow of Lena.

> The powerfully maternal Rinthy, hunting her "chap" and lactating helplessly, is of course a figure of great natural fecundity, the earth-as-mother who lies at the heart of the pastoral myth. Bell has pointed out that Rinthy is McCarthy's version of Lena Grove, Faulkner's footloose embodiment of the maternal (and pastoral, as her name implies) life force. But Rinthy is a dark and hopeless version of Lena, just as *Outer Dark*—the very title suggests it—is a dark and hopeless version of *Light in August*. (Grammer 38)[30]

Lena's positive maternal attributes are inverted into their worst possible counterimages. Rinthy's child is born not only out of wedlock but from an incestuous union. She is not just hunting the child's father but the child itself. While she too meets with hospitality she is invariably prevented from accepting it. Although she is courted by a farmer, as Lena is by Byron Bunch, she steals away from "the dead and loveless house" (211) in the night. Instead of interrupting her quest like Lena, she is doomed to perpetuate her hopeless errand. And rather than matching her peregrination with Lena's adventurousness, she roams the countryside as a wayward stray. "Lost, she said. Yes I'm lost" (58), whereas Lena marvels, "My, my. A body does get around" (*Light in August* 507).

In short, while Lena personifies the tranquil endurance of "pastoral stillness," Rinthy's grace is that of absolute abjection, and her refusal to overcome the loss of her child allegorizes the narrator's melancholia, as does Culla's refusal to confront his crisis. "Suffering unfurls its microcosm through the reverberations of characters. They are articulated as doubles, as in mirrors that magnify their melancholia to the point of violence and delirium" (Kristeva, *Sun* 257). Rinthy's stylization as a type becomes apparent whenever her movements are compared to the mechanical motions of a doll. Examples abound: In the scene of her departure "[s]he pirouetted slowly in the center of the room like a doll unwinding" (53). Other passages describe her as "doll-like" (210), as watching "with such doll's eyes of painted china" (24), and moving "like a crippled marionette" (32). To stylize Rinthy into an allegorical figure whose suffering shows as "something half wild in her look" (155), something "half deranged" (151), goes considerably further than Lena's portrayal as a realistic figure with allegorical aspects. A grotesque adaptation of Lena, Rinthy personifies the abjection of what is still quasi-virginal in Faulkner's pastoralism. It attests to McCarthy's craftsmanship that she seems nonetheless as real as she could not possibly be.

The principal difference between *Light in August* and *Outer Dark*, then, is not in essence but in degree of stylization and mood. Much the same can be said in regard to McCarthy's relationship to traditional Southern gothicism as a whole. That the myth of Southern pastoralism (as a literary cliché) constitutes the novel's true realm of the abject is illustrated by microcosmic instances such as the following, describing a still life of Southern pastoralism frozen in time and space: "People were moving from shade to shade beneath the store awnings and across the bright noon clay with leaden steps, moving beneath the blinding heat like toilers in a dream stunned and without purpose. The first man he came upon that was not caught up in this listless tableau was a teamster fitting a wheel" (134–35). The narrator's retrospective gaze here perceives the narrative present as an anachronism, as something that will always have already passed. Melancholy discourse is marked by its sense of monumental, mythic time, and when Bleikasten writes about *Light in August* that "Lena comes to us, comes back to us from the plumbless depths of a time before time, prior to the nightmare of history, a time slow and simple" (275) he also captures Rinthy: "Emaciate and blinking and with the wind among her rags she looked like something replevied by grim miracle from the ground and sent with tattered windings and halt corporeality into the agony of sunlight. Butterflies attended her and birds dusting in the road did not fly up when she passed. She hummed to herself as she went some child's song from an old dead time" (*Outer Dark* 97–98). Likened to a revenant, Rinthy simultaneously personifies pastoral abjection and pastoral bliss, and the discrepancy between the two extremes could hardly be greater.

Nor could the meta-narrative sense of loss ("an old dead time") be more specific, because the imagery of the passage, unwarranted by the context, suggests that not an intratextual past but the intertextual past (the literary imagination of the Southern pastoral) has become the object of retrospective fixation. What Kristeva writes about the melancholic's sense of time certainly applies to this and comparable emblems that inscribe melancholy retrospection into an allegorical pastiche of pastoral déjà vu: "As the time in which we live is the time of our discourse, the alien, retarded, or vanishing speech of melancholy people leads them to live within a skewed time sense. It does not pass by, the before/after notion does not rule it, does not direct it from a past toward a goal. . . . Riveted to the past, regressing to the paradise or inferno of an unsurpassable experience, melancholy persons manifest a strange memory: everything has gone by, they seem to say, but I am faithful to those bygone days, I am nailed down to them, no revolution is possible, there is no future" (*Sun* 60). McCarthy's work, which at first glance "seems to have very little to do with southern literary tradition" (Grammer 30), in fact constitutes a (con)temporary apex of that tradition.

Having reworked the Southern pastoral into a vision darker than the novel's literary antecedents by reproducing in it the narrator's, not just the characters', darkness of soul, *Outer Dark* takes the psychological tendency of the Faulkner tradition to extremes. It simultaneously transcends that literary tradition by reducing it to the function of a stage set on which the death of Southern pastoralism itself is dramatized. Unlike *The Orchard Keeper,* which develops an alternative sense of pastoral based on the desolation of the garden, and unlike *Child of God,* which proceeds from pastoral desolation to a positive wilderness ideal, *Outer Dark* lapses into absolute pastoral melancholia. The novel was written before *Child of God,* and in its reference to traditional Southern pastoralism it precedes McCarthy's wilderness turn, but its fierce allegoresis of melancholia proper groups it with *Blood Meridian,* in which the same mood is inspired by desert wilderness.

Yet the novel does not close on this plaintive note. *Outer Dark* couches its imagery of death and desolation in variations on the *vanitas* motif, which in baroque art was moralistic in the sense that its despondency included the hope for atonement and redemption. In its teleology, the baroque emblem serves a dogmatic function, and it finds its match in *Outer Dark*. In the novel, which is neither "brutally nihilistic" (Bell, *Achievement* 34) nor a "morality play" (Leiter 91), the hope for redemption depends on the enunciation of guilt. Arnold contends that "in McCarthy's highly moralistic world, sins must be named and owned before they can be forgiven" ("Naming" 54). It is within the power of allegory to name guilt.

On the one hand allegory aligns all text with the vanishing point of death, on the other hand it provides melancholia with a signifier that secures (discursive) survival for the melancholy subject. Culla's failure to face his complicity with evil constitutes the allegorical causation underlying the terrorism on the plot level,[31] but narration of his tale enables the narrator on the meta-narrative level to master his own abjection.

The sense of enunciation-as-redemption is strongest toward the end when the full measure of wrath has been exacted in the murder of tinker and child; when the avenging triune has vacated the pages; when "after a while little sister lay sleeping" (238) in the beatific scene in the glade; when the blind man's paradoxical observation that "it's good to see the sun again" (239) sounds a note of absolution for "that feller" (241) who is none other than Culla; and when even the tinker's skeleton transforms into an emblem of tranquillity and cosmic harmony.

> The tinker in his burial tree was a wonder to the birds. The vultures that came by day to nose with their hooked beaks among his buttons and pockets like outrageous pets soon left him naked of his rags and flesh alike. Black mandrake sprang beneath the tree as it will where the seed of the hanged falls and in spring a new branch pierced his breast and flowered in a green boutonniere perennial beneath his yellow grin. He took the sparse winter snows upon what thatch of hair still clung to his dried skull and hunters that passed that way never chanced to see him brooding among his barren limbs. Until wind had tolled the tinker's bones and seasons loosed them one by one to the ground below and alone his bleached and weathered brisket hung in that lonesome wood like a bone birdcage. (238)

As it signifies both redemption for the tinker and the restoration of pastoral harmony independent of the Southern locale (much like the graveyard scene in *The Orchard Keeper*), this subchapter stands out because it redirects the narrative gaze to a redemptive pastoralism older than Southern fiction. And so, telling his tale of rue enables the narrator of *Outer Dark*—committed at once to the pastoral world and to the melancholy abdication of it—to celebrate pastoral beauty on its dying day.

CHAPTER TWO

"Optical Democracy"

Biocentrism in *Blood Meridian* (1985)

> The desert says nothing. Completely passive, acted upon but never acting, the desert lies there like the bare skeleton of Being, spare, sparse, austere, utterly worthless, inviting not love but contemplation. In its simplicity and order it suggests the classical, except that the desert is a realm beyond the human and in the classicist view only the human is regarded as significant or even recognized as real.
>
> Edward Abbey, *Desert Solitaire*

The discussion of the dissemination of Southern pastoralism in *Outer Dark* and the discussion of the wilderness turn in *Child of God* lead directly to a pastoral reading of *Blood Meridian, or the Evening Redness in the West*, the keystone of McCarthy's oeuvre. To classify this work as a pastoral novel may seem questionable considering that the setting is the Southwestern desert. Yet *Blood Meridian* has already been subjected to several ecopastoral interpretations because the textual prominence of wilderness in any form is impossible to overlook. Both *Outer Dark* and *Child of God* pair a wild or melancholy psyche with a wild or melancholy landscape in order to envision a pastoral alternative. This trend culminates in *Blood Meridian* because here the absolute lawlessness of the characters matches the absolute wilderness of the setting. As in the other two novels, a melancholy narrator projects allegorical characters into a microcosmic landscape, and no approach other than an allegorical one will unite the novel's protagonists, plot action, and nature aesthetic in one homogeneous interpretation.

The story is simple and resembles a picaresque journey of sorts. The overture introduces the nameless protagonist, "the kid"—another one of McCarthy's homeless and uneducated teenage picaros—and narrates his flight out West and his adventures with a band of filibusters in the wake of the Mexican-American War of 1848. In the main part of the novel the kid signs up with a troop of brigands led by John Joel Glanton, contracting with Mexican state governors as headhunters against the Apaches. Without scruples he participates in the slaughter of any black-haired natives they find, a phase lasting about two years and terminating in the gang's annihilation by the Yuma on the Colorado River. In this part, where the unholy crusade turns into a sheer struggle for survival, carnage alternates with the monologues of Judge Holden, an albino of superhuman strength, erudition, and cruelty who emerges as a second protagonist. The third part fast-forwards through almost three decades up to the novel's denouement in Texas in 1878, where the kid meets again with the judge and dies at his hands. The judge, "a huge messianic figure, a kind of Ahab crossed with Conrad's Kurtz" (Aldridge 94), ends up being the sole survivor of the gang. A one-page epilogue concludes the novel with a parable on the frontier.

No one would dispute that the novel in some way discusses (similar to *Moby Dick*) westward expansion, American imperialism, and Social Darwinism. But historicist approaches to *Blood Meridian* depend on the textual surface for interpreting the characters and motives while they neglect the expository parts (especially the description of nature). By contrast, ecocritical interpretations, acknowledging the interdependence between the scalp hunters' progress and the judge's monologues on the one hand, and the dense descriptions of desert landscape on the other, have found the novel to be invested with a pastoral aesthetic. Hence, the focus here will rest on the book's anti-anthropocentric pastoralism that most ecocritically minded reviews identify.[1] In the context of a pastoral interpretation of the novel this means a privileging of the overtly allegorical first and third parts (which are markedly shorter than the bulk of the central part), as well as of the one-page italicized epilogue (recalling the emblematic prologue of *The Orchard Keeper*).

Because the dominant environment in *Blood Meridian* is clearly wilderness, the pastoral allegory reflecting the decline of the agrarian ideal with which it begins is easily overlooked. The setting of *Blood Meridian* is the "howling wilderness" (42) that has haunted the American imagination since Puritan times, though relocated in the Chihuahua desert. Yet the kid, like a true pastoral protagonist, passes first through an agrarian landscape—that of his native Tennessee—when running away from home: "He wanders west as far as Memphis, a solitary migrant upon that flat and pastoral landscape. Blacks in the fields, lank and stooped, their fingers spiderlike among the bolls of cotton. A shadowed agony in the garden. Against the sun's declining figures moving in the slower dusk across a paper skyline. A lone dark husbandman pursuing mule and harrow down the rainblown bottomland toward night" (4). As if to document the change of locale in McCarthy's work, the words "paper skyline" create a two-dimensional tableau of the cursed garden in the manner of McCarthy's Southern novels. The motif of the ruined garden is picked up again when the scalp hunters "passed abandoned haciendas and roadside graves" (226), "[m]ud pueblos that lay like plague towns with the crops rotting in the fields" (176), and "[e]mpty fields where the crops had rotted" (223). Before moving on to Texas, the kid stays long enough in New Orleans to experience the decadence associated in pastoral fiction with city life. Here, the same atmosphere of corruption prevails that later infuses the Fort Griffin episode. Following this interlude, the protagonist ships out to Texas, not quite yet reaching wilderness but a purgatorial frontier where "whores call to him from the dark like souls in want" (5), where "come days of begging, days of theft," and "where there rode no soul save he" (15).

As the novel progresses, the narrator's infatuation with the desert landscape makes it seem as if the very hostility of this environment accommodated McCarthy's wilderness pastoralism better than any other setting. Accordingly, the novel's phrase "optical democracy" comes to define the author's pastoral aesthetic:

> In the neuter austerity of that terrain all phenomena were bequeathed a strange equality and no one thing nor spider nor stone nor blade of grass could put forth claim to precedence. The very clarity of these articles belied their familiarity, for the eye predicates the whole on some feature or part and here was nothing more luminous than another and nothing more enshadowed and in the optical democracy of such landscapes all preference is made whimsical and a man and a rock become endowed with unguessed kinships." (247)[2]

This passage, among many others, has prompted Steven Shaviro to observe that in *Blood Meridian* "the prejudices of anthropocentric perceptions are disqualified. The eye no longer constitutes the axis of vision. We are given instead a kind of perception before or beyond the human" (153). James Lilley, expanding on Shaviro's observation, argues that McCarthy's "narrative voice always emphasizes the horizontal, physical, factualness of things, employing a startling array of precise nouns which shift the focus of the text away from any vertical, symbolic axis replete with hidden significance" (163). Lilley compares this kind of description with the landscape photography of Ansel Adams, among others: "In the same way that McCarthy's 'optically democratic' landscape obliterates the 'fog' that colors our representations of the environment, so too Group f/64 were eager to remove any focal point or 'depth' to their photography, thereby allowing the material essence of the natural world to manifest itself in the pictorial space. . . . The effect of such visual surface is, in both text and photograph, to highlight the sheer physicality, the horizontal 'factualness' and corporeality of nature" (164). David Holloway in turn endorses Lilley's point by tracing McCarthy's rhetoric back to "modernism's own search for 'the quintessence,' the unmediated moment of epiphany, when what is conceived to be the artifice of life is stripped away, and the inner natural essence of the 'thing itself' shines through" (195). In discussing the formal organization of this kind of rhetoric, Holloway differentiates between "optical democracy" as an ecopastoral aesthetic and the literary communication of this aesthetic. As he scrutinizes the syntax used in *Blood Meridian,* Holloway concludes that "optical democracy might be thought of as a series of prose forms which diminish language as an agency of human cognition, binding McCarthy's aesthetic ever more tightly to a phenomenal world upon which language might otherwise go to work" (192).

The formal peculiarity that Lilley identifies as "a startling array of precise nouns" (163) is further defined by Holloway as a technique by which "a proportion of the individual nouns that accumulate in any given passage are laced together with their own verbs and adjectives" in order to focus the point of view on the "phenomenological exclusivity of the objects described" (194). Holloway cites the following passage to illustrate how the narrator of *Blood Meridian* relies heavily on the use of similes that do not just operate as similes but accumulate until all narrative detail seems to be equidistant from the reader in a "superabundance of objects on view" (194):

> They rode for days through the rain and they rode through rain and hail and rain again. In that gray storm light they crossed a flooded plain with the footed shapes of the horses reflected in the water among clouds and mountains and the riders slumped forward and rightly

> skeptic of the shimmering cities on the distant shore of that sea whereon they trod miraculous. They climbed up through rolling grasslands where small birds shied away chittering down the wind and a buzzard labored up from among bones with wings that went whoop whoop whoop like a child's toy swung on a string and in the long red sunset the sheets of water on the plain below lay like tidepools of primal blood. (186–87)

Here, an interminable trek through steady rain is placed side by side (not juxtaposed) with momentary impressions such as bird sounds and the ascent of a buzzard. The sheer materiality of things (water, grassland, bones) alternates with imaginary impressions (the mirage, the associations of blood and toy). What the narration achieves by foregoing the use of sub-clauses and proper punctuation is a suspension of temporal and spatial definition that recalls the effect of parataxis discussed above. The narration proceeds in a manner almost cinematographic—frame by frame, pan altering with zoom, alternating angles—retarding the interpretative function of the narrator: plain, horse shapes, riders, fata morgana, grasslands, birds, single bird, flooded plain. Phillips argues that the syntax of *Blood Meridian* overcomes the limits of perspective "as if the sentence had been written by a transparent eyeball that has learned how not to be Emersonian" ("History" 447). Interestingly, Craig Owens elaborates the kinship of allegorical to cinematographic imagery at the same time that he classifies the Western generically as allegory: "The Western, the gangster saga, science fiction—these are the allegories of the twentieth century. They are also genres most intimately associated with film; that film should be the primary vehicle for modern allegory may be attributed not only to its unquestioned status as the most popular of contemporary art forms, but also to its mode of representation. Film composes narratives out of a succession of concrete images, which makes it particularly suited to allegory's essential pictogrammatism" (230). The following example of the novel's use of microcosmic emblems illustrates how the choppy syntax of "film stills" narration neutralizes narrative distance to the point of indiscriminateness. The technique implies an egalitarian intention on a secondary level, which again is an allegorical one. This metanarrative emerges as the perspective shifts from the riders' progress to one rider, to an object, to his reflection on the object, back to the riders progress, to their environment, to a deadly confrontation without having built up to it:

> They rode on into the mountains and their way took them through high pine forests, wind in the trees, lonely birdcalls. The shoeless mules slaloming through the dry grass and pine needles. In the blue coulees on the north slopes narrow tailings of old snow. They rode up switchbacks through a lonely aspen wood where the fallen leaves lay like golden disclets in the damp black trail. The leaves shifted in a million spangles down the pale corridors and Glanton took one and turned it like a tiny fan by its stem and held it and let it fall and its perfection was not lost on him. They rode through a narrow draw where the leaves were shingled up in ice and they crossed a high saddle at sunset where wild doves were rocketing down the wind and passing through the gap a few feet off the ground, veering wildly among the ponies and dropping off down into the blue gulf beyond. They rode on into a dark fir forest, the little Spanish ponies sucking at the thin air, and just at dusk as Glanton's horse was clambering over a fallen log a lean blond bear rose up out of the swale on the far side where it had been feeding and looked down at them with dim pig's eyes. (136–37)

Out of the seven sentences of this paragraph, four start with reiterations of "They rode." Two of the three remaining sentences are grammatically incomplete and should be sub-clauses of the preceding sentence. Although the scalp hunters are introduced as the grammatical subject in most clauses, the sentences are so devoted to the contemplation of nature that even the clause describing Glanton's scrutiny of the aspen leaf ties his personal reflection into the narrative (very human, if not anthropocentric) contemplation of material nature. As it allocates equal syntactic valence for all subjects, the narrative voice insinuates the existential equality of humans, domestic animals, wild animals, and inanimate nature. Consequently, the confrontation with the bear—despite its sense of drama—is not privileged over the contemplation of the aspen leaf.

Passages such as this one—eroding anthropocentric meaning—abound in *Blood Meridian*. In the passage following the excerpt, the bear slays a man who is one of the Delaware trackers. The narrative voice proceeds to discuss the Delaware gang members who paradoxically stalk other representatives of their own ethnic group, and the narration would threaten to become epigonic if its effect was not so clearly calculated. As becomes obvious in the subsequent quote, these killers share in an absolute degree of wildness with bear and land and even the wind. Nor does the narrator differentiate between physical and mental landscape, between this incident and an entire history of such incidents, between the individual and the species:

> Nothing moved in that high wilderness save the wind. They did not speak. They were men of another time for all that they bore christian names and they had lived all their lives in a wilderness as had their fathers before them. They'd learnt war by warring, the generations driven from the eastern shore across a continent, from the ashes at Gnadenhutten onto the prairies and across the outlet to the bloodlands of the west. If much in the world were mystery the limits of that world were not, for it was without measure or bound and there were contained within it creatures more horrible yet and men of other colors and beings which no man has looked upon and yet not alien none of it more than were their own hearts alien in them, whatever wilderness contained there and whatever beast. (138)

The technique underlying the novel's egalitarian aesthetic is to elevate nature—as in *Child of God*—to an existential rank equal to that of human beings. The intention is to identify a wild element, and a concomitant wilderness ethos, on all levels of existence. As exposition (of setting and character) assumes the same status as plot action, the aesthetic leveling is necessarily effected at the expense of the protagonists' status. Recalling the interpretation of *Outer Dark,* it is safe to say that the characters of *Blood Meridian* too are reduced to types. The protagonists' de-individualized status becomes even more obvious in the desert scenes. Nowhere in McCarthy's work is the resistance of wilderness to the logocentric encoding of nature as a cultural artifact more patent, more successful. In the quote below, reason and culture are explicitly erased by the wildness of landscape:[3] "The desert upon which they were entrained was desert absolute and it was devoid of feature altogether and there was nothing to mark their progress upon it. The earth fell away on every side equally in its arcature and by these limits were they circumscribed and of them were they locus" (295–96).

The "optical democracy" of expository narration is complemented by the structuring of plot action. The tendency to divest the characters of individuality and agency can also be observed in the interaction between them, such as when the point of view shifts three times within a single sentence: "He sees a parricide hanged in a crossroads hamlet and the man's friends run forward and pull his legs and he hangs dead from his rope while urine darkens his trousers" (5). The tendency becomes even more patent in the numerous battle scenes, where human cognition informs a given point of view but narration is not attributable to the subject named. Instead, the images flood the pages intellectually unprocessed. Thomas Pughe argues that even and especially scenes of bloodshed are narrated in unreflective, paratactic word clusters that are "not only cut off from individual experience but also from the historical context" (374), and that "McCarthy's narrator thus interposes himself between the fictional world and the reader, frustrating 'identification' in an historical as well as in an emotional sense" (375). Pughe cites the "wild frieze" (*Blood Meridian* 53) of the Comanche attack to compare this narrative effect to the neutral vision of a film-camera insofar as the scalp hunters are represented as nonhistorical beings, devoid of agency, and insofar as "human civilization disappears into nature" in "this transhistorical vision" (378). The same transhistorical perspective is applied to the kid very early in the novel: "His origins are become remote as is his destiny and not again in all the world's turning will there be terrains so wild and barbarous to try whether the stuff of creation may be shaped to man's will or whether his own heart is not another kind of clay" (4–5).

Passages of this kind—when read in conjunction with the novel's wilderness discourse and its typological reduction of characters—identify the pastoral intention of *Blood Meridian* as the suspension of the human claim to stewardship over nature. This claim underlies the pastoralism of the humanist "subject that only speaks soliloquies in a world of irrational silences" (Manes 25). In the book, it is epitomized in the figure of Glanton, who "was equal to whatever might follow for he was complete at every hour" and had "long foresworn all weighing of consequence and . . . usurped to contain within him all that he would ever be in this world and all that the world would be to him" (243).[4] In the course of the narrative, Glanton's proto-fascist personality confronts, and is erased by, the totalitarian ecosphere of the desert, lethal and silent. He is a rash psychopath radically at odds with the wilderness he picks as his domain. Glanton, who goes insane during his Faustian quest in the wilderness,[5] represents a schizoid self to whom the words of the epigraph by Paul Valéry apply: "Finally you fear blood more and more. Blood and time."

In its post-humanist, "optically democratic" representation of wilderness, *Blood Meridian* undertakes to imagine nature in its sheer materiality, beyond anthropocentric terms. The novel's narrative thrust ultimately renders the desert hostile to human signification altogether, so that the silent deadliness of the ecotope becomes generally emblematic of the silence of death.[6] This aesthetic effect resembles in fiction what Phillips has called "a truly materialist version—ecologically rather than economically based—of 'cognitive mapping,' which must entail wiping our fingerprints off the landscape as we redraw the maps in our minds" ("Nature" 219). The object of "cognitive mapping" is to overcome the technological view of nature as "a potential human artifact" (Phillips, "Nature" 218). Such biocentric remapping is undertaken in *Blood Meridian* wherever the wilderness setting is represented in terms of absence, that is, as being silent and voided:[7] "There is hardly in the world a waste so barren but some creature will not cry out at night, yet here one was and they listened to their breathing in the dark and the cold and they listened to the systole of the rubymeated hearts that hung within them" (281). The emptiness and silence of the desert landscape is quintessential for an ecocritical interpretation of *Blood Meridian*. As Christopher Manes writes, "Nature *is* silent in our culture (and in literate societies generally) in the sense that the status of being a speaking subject is jealously guarded as an exclusively human prerogative" (15). Manes elaborates how the humanist episteme "with its faith in reason, intellect and progress, has created an immense realm of silences, a world of 'not saids' called nature" (17), that in its eerie inarticulateness "surrounds our garrulous human subjectivity" (16).

While the anthropocentric view of nature provokes an ecocritical counter-ethic, Manes concedes that an antirationalist approach might be viewed as a totalitarian privileging of nature's irrationality. The suspicion that biocentrism is as totalitarian as it seems egalitarian becomes readily apparent when the desert subjects the Glanton gang to its optical democracy (rather than being subjected to human domination) to the point where the gang members too have become feral, lethal, totalitarian, thoroughly adapted to the ecosphere they inhabit. "Haggard and haunted and blacked by the sun. . . . Even the horses looked alien to any he'd ever seen, decked as they were in human hair and teeth and skin. Save for their guns and buckles and a few pieces of metal in the harness of the animals there was nothing about these arrivals to suggest even the discovery of the wheel" (232). As human efforts are implicated in the timeless materiality of nature, it would seem plausible if the reflection of the futility of human efforts were to occasion sorrow. Instead, the narrative realization of humanity's true existential status in the wilderness is undertaken without the use of elegiac language. The equalizing effect of the silence of nature (reflected in the de-individualized characters, though not in the narrative consciousness) is neither countermanded by a new land ethic nor lamented as being inhuman.

In *Outer Dark*, the silence of nature is invoked in great descriptive detail and through allegoresis. There, silent nature serves as a reflection of meta-narrative melancholia, though it does not inspire lamentation over the loss of human stewardship over nature. *Blood Meridian* goes a step farther, because here the silence of nature is foregrounded not to allegorize the melancholia of the speaking human subject. Instead, the melancholia inspired by the silence of nature motivates the dissemination of the anthropocentric human subject. In a way, the Western landscape in *Blood Meridian* continues to function as a *paysage moralisé* (as it does in Albert Bierstadt's paintings and Zane Grey's novels), but instead of reflecting societal morality for the benefit of themselves, the narrator, or readers, the characters reflect the wilderness ethos of survivalism as dictated by the desert.

The survival instinct substitutes for virtue in an animistic land ethic that ignores every metaphysical tenet except the respect for all life. It thus represents a third or trivial moral alternative (and is in essence no morality at all). This survivalist wilderness ethos finds its apotheosis in the emblem of the burning tree, where the phrase "precarious truce" becomes as programmatic as the phrase "optical democracy." The individuality of the human figure is inscribed only by the word "solitary," and only in regard to human company. The adjective "heraldic" manifests the tree's emblematic quality:

> It was a lone tree burning on the desert. A heraldic tree that the passing storm had left afire. The solitary pilgrim drawn up before it had traveled far to be here and he knelt in the hot sand and held his numbed hands out while all about in that circle attended companies of lesser auxiliaries routed forth into the inordinate day, small owls that crouched silently and stood from foot to foot and tarantulas and solpugas and vinegarroons and the vicious mygale spiders and beaded lizards with mouths black as a chowdog's, deadly to man, and the little desert basilisks that jet blood from their eyes and the small sandvipers like seemly gods, silent and the same, in Jeda, in Babylon. A constellation of ignited eyes that edged the ring of light all bound in a precarious truce before this torch whose brightness had set back the stars in their sockets. (215)[8]

Among other typological connotations, this passage obviously refers back to the burning bush out of which God advises Moses that he is standing on sacred ground (Exod. 3:5). It is in respect to such moments that Phillips argues, "[D]escription and the natural world as categories contain both narrative and human beings. Human beings and the natural world do not figure as antagonists—*Blood Meridian* does not have that kind of dramatic structure. They are instead parts of the same continuum and are consistently described by McCarthy as such" ("History" 446). The indifference toward individual biography and human sensibility that these moments communicate can be unsettling: "It is precisely its lack of human implication that some find *Blood Meridian*'s most disturbing feature. In the raw orchestration of the book's events, the world of nature and the world of men are parts of the same world, and both are equally violent and indifferent to the other" ("History" 447). Despite its nature mysticism, *Blood Meridian* contains not even the hope for secular transcendence into a pastoral utopia, no trace of pastoral escapism. In this sense, the novel constitutes the nadir of McCarthy's evolving pastoralism, being even more hopeless in its vision of pastoral desolation than *Outer Dark*. Not until *All the Pretty Horses* does a note of pastoral optimism reemerge.

Yet the egalitarianism of the Border Trilogy presupposes the allegorical destruction of pastoral anthropocentrism *in Blood Meridian*. It presupposes the leveling effect of universal mortality. And it also presupposes the melancholy equanimity that pastoral desolation inspires in the narrative consciousness, and that is expressed in the novel's second epigraph by the baroque mystic Jacob Boehme (1575–1624): "There is no sorrowing. For sorrow is a thing that is swallowed up in death, and death and dying are the very life of darkness." This aptly captures the state of mind of the narrator, who seeks to inscribe the ability to survive—the principal ecopastoral ideal—in the figure of the picaro, but instead locates an absolute existential tenacity in the materiality of the desert landscape and in death itself.

Both the picaresque novel and the Western are allegorical genres preoccupied with survival in the hostile environments of society or wilderness, respectively. *Blood Meridian* features elements of both genres; it is a picaresque Western. Any discussion of the survival theme will have to hinge on the figure of the kid, who is clearly marked by the picaro's social deracination, what with his dead mother, alcoholic father, and his elopement at age fourteen. Joseph Meeker's summary of the picaro describes him perfectly: "The picaro's birth is generally obscure, often illegitimate, suggesting both his lack of social status and the absence of any sense of continuity with the past. The chaotic social environment in which he grows up has no niche prepared for him, and he soon discovers that he must create whatever success he can from the rawest of materials at hand. Early in life he goes on his own" (59). More important than his uprooted state, the kid shows the trickster's aptitude for survival, a skill that includes his willingness to serve any master or institution as long as doing so will help him get by. He serves in turn Captain White, Captain Glanton, a pack train conductor, and a farmer, and works in "different trades" (312), at a sawmill and even at "a diphtheria pesthouse" (5). Nowhere does he stay for long, and never does he commit himself to the social order, for "[t]he picaro is an outsider to this system, practical, clever, amoral, self-sufficient, and dedicated to making do by the best means available. Staying alive is his most important purpose, and having a good time comes second" (Meeker 60). The kid's lack of zeal for the Glanton Gang's genocidal mission earns him the epithet "mutinous" by the judge: "No assassin, called the judge. And no partisan either" (299). The picaro's response to "the omnipresent threat of injury and death" is to "[a]dapt to circumstances and take evasive action" (Meeker 61).

Eventually, however, the kid falls victim to the judge. The judge in turn represents a type in direct opposition to the picaresque type, and the typological opposition is best explained with the dualism of Senex and Puer in Jungian psychology. Within Jung's dualism of archetypes, the patriarchal type of the Senex stands in juxtaposition to the picaresque type of the Puer who signifies youth and its attendant attributes, such as revolt, transcendence, idealization, and the crossing of boundaries. The Puer represents childhood less than "the Divine Child, the figures of Eros, . . . the Trickster, and the Messiah" (Hillman 23), and arguably the kid represents the counterpart to the judge's dominant Senex persona. That the picaresque protagonist emulates the archetype of the Puer is also suggested by the fact that he remains nameless. "Kid" practically translates into the Latin "puer," and within the narrative, the terms "the kid" and "the judge" are used to refer to these two types rather than—as proper names would—to fictional characters in the usual sense.

The figure of the picaro is of great interest in the ecopastoral context of *Blood Meridian* because the picaresque tradition, understood as "a mode of survival against odds in a world that is hostile or indifferent" (Meeker 51), interacts with the pastoral theme of the novel insofar as the societal environment of the Wild West coexists with the natural environment of desert wilderness. Meeker outlines the kinship between the picaresque and pastoral genres: "Simply put, escape from the mad world or adaptation to its condition are the choices offered by the pastoral or picaresque modes. Both presuppose some necessary relationship between human social and biological environments, but differ in their assessment of that relationship. The pastoral looks longingly at biological nature as an alternative to society, while the picaresque sees society itself as a natural environment—a wilderness" (51). Moreover, Meeker points out, "War is often the setting for picaresque novels because its conditions intensify the problems to which the picaro must always adapt himself: rapid change, social disorder, irrationality, and constant threat of injury or death" (62–63). The anomy manifest in landscape and society in *Blood Meridian* provides a picaresque setting of extreme direness. Yet what makes the figure of the picaro most interesting for an ecocritical reading is that his emphasis on survival represents a comic approach to life. This approach stands juxtaposed to the tragic ordering of the cosmos into finite categories. "Both tragedy and comedy arise from experiences of misfortune, but they respond to pain in different ways." For the ecopastoral context, Meeker characterizes the humanist ideal of the tragic way as a dead-ended framework of dichotomies, "a pattern that Western culture has developed over many centuries to deal with loss, grief, and death": "The tragic way is to locate suffering according to a polarized idea of contrasts: good and evil, light and dark, God and the Devil, truth and falsehood, male and female, friend and enemy. Tragedy occurs when one makes a commitment to the positive end of the polar pair, then suffers from the corresponding negative end." Consequently, the tragic drama tends to end in a denouement of resounding finality "to show that a sequence of willed events has led to its ultimate consequence" (Meeker 14). Comic narratives—picaresque ones among them—remain open-ended, conciliatory, inclusive, and playful: "The comic way, on the other hand, is the path of reconciliation. When the usual patterns of life are disrupted, the comic spirit strives for a return to normalcy. The comic vision is not polarized, but complex: comedy sees many aspects simultaneously, and seeks for a strategy that will resolve problems with a minimum of pain and confrontation. The comic way is not heroic or idealistic; rather, it is a strategy for survival" (Meeker 14–15). Meeker's somewhat reductive argument is relevant in that it applies not just to the composition of *Blood Meridian* but to that of McCarthy's work as a whole. All of McCarthy's books are picaresque novels, all of them are inconclusive, conciliatory in a biocentric sense, and preoccupied with the survival of outsiders in non-heroic ways. The only metaphysical or ideological paradigm the author endorses is wilderness animism. Even the judge's soliloquies represent an animistic adaptation of gnostic notions. Much of what happens in *Blood Meridian* defies both reason and morality, and again Meeker's theory applies: "Comedy literally has no use for morality, for moral insights play no significant role in the comic experience. Similarly, comedy normally avoids strong emotions.

Passionate love, hate, or patriotism generally appear ridiculous in a comic context, for comedy tends to generate a psychological mood that is incompatible with deep emotions. Great ideas and ideals fare no better at the hands of comedy, which ordinarily treats them as if they were insignificant" (15). The kid's comment regarding a head that has been preserved in alcohol substantiates this notion: "Somebody ought to have pickled it long time ago. By rights they ought to pickle mine. For taking up with such a fool." His reaction is matched by the ironic inflection of the narrative voice: "It was Captain White. Lately at war among the heathen" (70).

What Meeker labels "the tragic view of life" must enter into the discussion of *Blood Meridian* as it depends on an anthropocentric attitude toward nature, and as "literary tragedy and environmental exploitation in Western culture share many of the same philosophical presuppositions." Meeker identifies the tragic way as "a cultural invention" of Western civilization, "with no true counterpart in primitive or Oriental cultures": "Three such ideas will illustrate the point: the assumption that nature exists for the benefit of humanity, the belief that human morality transcends natural limitations, and humanism's insistence upon the supreme importance of the individual personality. All are characteristic beliefs that appear implicitly and explicitly in tragic literature" (24). As these ideas are contested, subverted or ignored by the egalitarian composition of *Blood Meridian* in favor of open-endedness, continuity, and post-humanism, the narrative biocentrism of "optical democracy" manifests the "strategic" and "systemic" qualities (Meeker 17) of comic writing. The comic way expresses itself in the emblems of dance and play, such as they occur most prominently in the judge's monologues. Meeker writes that, unlike finite, tragic games (which result in victory and defeat), "Infinite play is a manifestation of the comic way. It can be found in the play of children and of animals, in enduring love, in evolution and natural selection, in symbiosis and cooperations of all kinds" (17–18). Games are marked by their non-object-oriented playfulness, spontaneity, and non-competitive creativity, not by conquest and death. The playfulness of the comic way constitutes the realm of the trivial, the third path that leads beyond to victory or defeat, and that promises survival. The picaro or trickster represents its master player.

All this relates to the discussion of the kid, because the kid's disinterested playing and the simultaneous playfulness of the judge undermine the ideal of the picaro's survival. Meeker writes that "the world itself can be our gigantic playground" (19), and the wilderness world of *Blood Meridian* does resemble a vast playground for the game of life whose boon is survival. But its principal player, the kid, pales by comparison to the one player who survives all and dances off the novel's last page in monstrous mimicry of the comic way; namely, the judge. In the course of the narrative, the judge emerges more and more as the true trickster figure. It is the judge who acknowledges play as the supreme and truest strategy of survival: "Men are born for games. Nothing else. Every child knows that play is nobler than work" (249). As he purposefully confuses the comic way (which is trivial) with the tragic way (which is noble), he perverts the systemic, productive concept of play into the very shadow of itself, that is, into the idea of universal warfare: "He loves games? Let him play for stakes" (147). The stakes and game he defines are sinister inversions of the comic play ethic, while representing a radicalization of anthropocentrism (and the tragic way) into something transcending human limitations: "Games of chance require a wager to have meaning at all. Games of sport involve the skill and strength of the opponents and the humiliation of defeat and the pride of victory are in themselves sufficient stake because they inhere in the worth of the principals and define them. But trial of chance or trial of worth all games aspire to the condition of war for here that which is wagered swallows up game, player, all" (249). Just as he understands war to be the game that subsumes all games, the judge allegorizes life into a dance of death subsuming all dances. He says so to the kid in the concluding chapter, which is so deeply allegorical as to resemble a fable. The kid listens to his enigmatic pronouncements as if in a trance, thus vindicating the judge's very words. His lack of interest even in the face of his foretold death is symptomatic of his indifference throughout. As the novel is told from *his* point of view and thus channels the narrative gaze, his indifference even regarding his own death reflects the abjection of not just his figure but of the narrative consciousness itself.[9] In *Blood Meridian* then, the comic way of the picaresque genre is undercut even as it visualizes an uncultivated world (wilderness) and a cultureless society (the Wild West) as a playground of survivalism. The novel manages to balance the interrelationship between man and nature at its lowest common denominator, that of survival. The narrative ecosystem of wilderness that is thus created resembles not the primitive state restored but absolute desolation.

The picaro's failure in *Blood Meridian* reflects the text's skepticism toward its own ecopastoral vision and may thus explain the underlying melancholy mood. Narrative melancholia and ambiguity toward biocentric notions infuse the text from the start, though they do not emerge until late in the story. Throughout much of the text the kid's survival skills seem awesome. They compile into a record of picaresque recklessness that is questionable only inasmuch as the kid seems all too willing to risk his life. At age fifteen "he is shot . . . just below the heart" (4) and heals up within two weeks; toward the end he is pierced by an arrow and recovers. He survives attacks by the Comanches, the Apaches, the Yumas, the Mexican Army. He makes his way out of the desert twice. He remains unscathed by incarceration in both Mexico and California. He shoots Apaches "as if he'd done it all before in a dream" (109). Even his wariness of the judge never solidifies into alarm, as his incautious inquiry "What's he a judge of?" (135) illustrates. He shrugs off Tobin's warning not to walk out to the judge at night, saying, "You think I'm afraid of him?" (219). Even at age forty-five, he warns Elrod's kin, "I see him back here I'll kill him" (322), and he is true to his word. Adept at surviving, he feels nothing but contempt for hapless people like Sproule, who is dying of consumption and gangrene: "I know your kind, he said. What's wrong with you is wrong all the way through you" (66). To Shelby's remark "This is a terrible place to die in" he answers unfazed, "Where is a good one?" (208).

The one time he shows fear is when—imprisoned and wounded—he is visited by the judge: "The kid stood with his back to the wall" (307). In the same subchapter he seems for the first time to be openly out of touch with his picaresque role model (at the same time coming closest to showing the emotional features of an individual's personality), speaking "with a strange urgency" (305). Early on in the novel, the narrator hints that the kid seems lifeless and might be victim more than perpetrator: "The child's face is curiously untouched behind the scars, the eyes oddly innocent" (4). "He keeps from off the king's road for fear of citizenry" (15). After the fight in the mud puddle in Nacogdoches the text suggests that Toadvine "looked like a great clay voodoo doll made animate and the kid looked like another" (13). It thus likens them to the figure of the Golem,[10] an android brought to life by magic but intrinsically lifeless. The tarot card assigned to the kid by the gypsy woman, "[c]uatro de copas" (94), is the same "gypsy card that was the four of cups" (59) that he found pasted to a wall earlier. The divinatory meaning of the card is "[w]eariness, disgust, aversion, imaginary vexations, as if the wine of this world had caused satiety only; another wine, as if a fairy gift, is now offered him but he sees no consolation therein."[11] For the kid, the card bespeaks bitter experience and "a divided heart." Sepich suggests, "The presence of this card in the novel as the kid's emblem is an appropriate validation of the judge's otherwise inexplicable accusations of the kid's 'clemency for the heathen'" (107). Rather than merciful, the kid seems too indifferent to be merciless, for his failure to kill the wounded Shelby in face of the advancing enemy is hardly charity. His lack of predatory zeal makes for the "flawed place in the fabric of your heart" (299).

The archetypal dualism in *Blood Meridian* is expressed in the judge's words to the kid: "Our animosities were formed and waiting before ever we two met." Yet the judge's very next line suggests that the kid is the heir apparent and disciple to the judge's dominion: "Yet even so you could have changed it all" (307). The same meaning probably underlies the judge's enigmatic remark to the kid that "some are not yet born who shall have cause to curse the Dauphin's soul," for the kid—"[t]he last of the true. The last of the true" (327)—will not take up what the judge calls "that higher calling which all men honor" (250), meaning war. This lack of dedication to an absolute dialectic is what the judge accuses him of, not moral qualms or mercy: "I spoke in the desert for you and you only and you turned a deaf ear to me. If war is not holy man is nothing but antic clay" (307). Indifferent to the point of suicide, the kid doctors Brown's leg when no one else will (162); he fetches water right before the eyes of the judge, who has by then become his enemy (285); and, all too indifferent, he declines to shoot the judge when opportunities present themselves (285, 298). Nor does he flee the saloon at Fort Griffin to save himself after the judge has virtually told him to his face that he will be sacrificed.[12]

A clue regarding the kid's negative adaptation of the picaro is provided by the fact that his ability to survive is most necessitated by his own predilection for fighting and his "taste for mindless violence" (3), that is, an auto-aggressive tendency tantamount to a death wish. Having run away to New Orleans, he frequents a tavern solely "to fight with the sailors" (4); at Nacogdoches he fights Toadvine over the rights to a boardwalk (9), then helps him to set fire to the hotel and beat a stranger senseless, no questions asked (12–13). At San Antonio de Bexar he challenges an entire cantina and kills the barman over his refusal to serve him (25). He joins the filibusters out of indecision and against a preacher's warning not to "carry war of a madman's making onto a foreign land. Ye'll wake more than dogs" (40).

The same self-destructive energy drives Glanton's desperados as a group, for they continue their rampage until they are themselves massacred by the Yuma in reciprocation of their own violence, that is, in much the same way they massacred the Gileños and the Tiguas earlier. At one point, black Jackson expresses the conviction "that he that lives by the sword shall perish by the sword" (248), and he clearly speaks for the whole gang. Moreover, certain apocalyptic descriptions of desert sun and Western sky structurally attend the kid's or the gang's progress as a suicidal quest for death on the blood meridian. "The sun to the west lay in a holocaust" (105) or "sat squat and pulsing and malevolent behind them" (45); "the enormous sun . . . sat boiling on the edge of the desert" (207), while "to the west lay reefs of bloodred clouds" (21), and "the western sky was the color of blood" (152).

The link between sunset and violent death, apparent in these quotes, is made explicit in the characterization of the Diegueños, who "knew that nothing excepting some savage pursuit could drive men to such plight and they watched each day for that thing to gather itself out of its terrible incubation in the house of the sun and . . . whether it be armies or plague or pestilence or something altogether unspeakable they waited with a strange equanimity" (300–301). There is a marked difference between these Native Americans and the desperados. Representing a collective of deindividualized, ecopastoral lifestyle, the Diegueños are invested with the same indifference the wilderness displays toward individual death. By contrast, the members of the Glanton Gang are invested with a willful auto-aggression that supersedes the urge for self-preservation. In the sense that they partake of the kid's violent self-abjection, the gang members function as allegorical subcharacters to the kid's archetype. The following quote insinuates a shared death wish: "Within a week of their quitting the city there would be a price of eight thousand pesos posted for Glanton's head. They rode out on the north road as would parties bound for [the safety of] El Paso but before they were even quite out of sight of the city they had turned their *tragic* mounts to the west and they rode *infatuate* and *half fond* toward the *red demise* of that day, toward the *evening lands* and the distant *pandemonium* of the sun" (185; emphases and parentheses added). Emblematic of the gang, the kid manifests an alienation and restlessness that go beyond the generic parameters of the picaro: "He traveled about from place to place" (312) until his death. He feels estranged even within the gang who "stared balefully at the kid as if he were no part of them for all they were so alike in wretchedness of circumstance" (218).

The total alienation and self-abjection that the kid manifests as a failed picaro on the plot level confirms his typological role on the meta-level. He represents the dejected type of whom Kristeva writes that "the deject is in short a *stray*. He is on a journey, during the night, the end of which keeps receding. He has a sense of the danger, of the loss that the pseudo-object attracting him represents for him, but he cannot help taking the risk at the very moment he sets himself apart" (*Horror* 8).[13] The horrifying tally of the kid's "mindless violence" cannot mitigate, nor can his nomadic roaming obliterate, the primal loss that traumatizes him. By contrast, the judge, who monopolizes the gang's (and in a way the novel's) discourse, comes to personify the symbolic order abjected by the narrative sense of self. Simultaneously the judge assumes the function of the subconscious in his childlike aspects.

The child imagery is of key importance. The novel opens with the strange *ecce homo* motif "See the child" (3, see Schopen 180), which refers to a context larger than the nameless protagonist who ceases to be "the child" on the second page.[14] Images of children or childishness recur throughout the novel independent of the protagonist, so that the child imagery constitutes in fact a central allegorical theme in *Blood Meridian*. Among the most haunting of the references to infancy is the following *nature morte* (or, still life):

> The way narrowed through rocks and by and by they came to a bush that was hung with dead babies.
>
> They stopped side by side, reeling in the heat. These small victims, seven, eight of them, had holes punched in their underjaws and were hung so by their throats from

> the broken stobs of a mesquite to stare eyeless at the naked sky. Bald and pale and bloated, larval to some unreckonable being. The castaways hobbled past, they looked back. Nothing moved. (57)[15]

This surreal vignette is neither anticipated by the context, nor elaborated, nor ever taken up again. It stands in structural isolation as an emblem that defies contextual interpretation, invested with the equalizing silence of nature ("Nothing moved" and "listening to the silence"). More importantly, the episode constitutes a nexus between the biocentric characterization of landscape (and the figures in it) and the narrator's abjection of the pastoral sense of self. Despite their realistic depiction, this nexus identifies the characters as allegorical figures of a pastoralism that has shifted from anthropocentrism to biocentrism.

That the still life of the bush hung with infant bodies functions as an emblem rather than a symbol is obvious, because an interpretation of the image in symbolical terms would be hard-pressed to match signifier (the image) with a specific signified or even an objective referent. What could it possibly signify inside a revisionist Western, except perhaps the cruelty of ethnic cleansing? The dead babies do not lend themselves to symbolic divination because—being out of context as they are—they carry no semantic weight outside the textual moment. Traversing the "optically democratic" narrative desert, in which all things are of equal importance and human constructs such as morality and aesthetics have no dominion, the reader stumbles upon a passage that would have to be considered morally and aesthetically shocking in terms of subject matter, and the question that presents itself and puts McCarthy's technique to the test is, which of the effects is more powerful: the moral outrageousness or the fact that the context renders moral outrage pointless?

Read as an image, the bush suggests typological references to literary precursors. Beatrice Trotignon reads "this passage as a reference to the 13th canto in Dante's *Inferno,* in which the souls of suicides are transformed into bushes on which their corpses are hung." The essential aspect of Trotignon's argument is that she classifies the image as typological: "McCarthy might not be referring to Dante, but this bush certainly belongs to the recognizable iconographic and literary descriptions of Hell in the Middle Ages, whether *Tungsdale's Vision* or Bosch's paintings. I refer you to the . . . detail of Bosch's Triptych ["The Garden of Delights"] representing three men impaled on a bush. However, these cultural icons belonged to a consensual and clearly defined theological typology" (4).[16] While the image in itself translates into an emblem of the predatory wilderness (human and natural) that the kid and Sproule traverse, and of nature's silence in humanist discourse, the typological intertextuality identifies the image as a reference to suicides and thus to melancholy abjection. The terrible vignette of the bush hung with dead infants, then, becomes an emblem of suicidal melancholia, and so identifies the structural function of the infant icon as being allegorical of the same narrative melancholia that was already diagnosed in McCarthy's earlier novels.

Thus, the novel's strange first line—"See the child"—assumes ominous importance, an importance highlighted by the incongruence of the passage.[17] For if "See the child" was to define the character first introduced as the protagonist, it would hardly designate him as "child" and then drop the term after two pages. If it was to draw attention to that person's childhood, the biblical rhetoric of the opening line would be out of place. In fact, the exhortation would seem justifiable only if it referred to something more than the kid's childhood and to someone other than the child he ceases to be on the very next page. As it instructs the reader from the start to watch for a de-individualized, typological child figure, the line "See the child" refers to the meaning of the child image as an emblem of prenatal existence—without identity yet but in unity with the maternal body—whose irredeemable loss haunts the melancholy psyche and inspires fantasies of violence.

Images of infanticide abound in *Blood Meridian*. One of the earliest instances involves the kid who with a rock "dropped a small child cleanly from the wall with no sound other than the muted thud of its landing on the far side" (71). Later, the desperados come across the site of a massacre, "the bones and skulls scattered along the bench for half a mile and the tiny limbs and toothless paper skulls of infants like the ossature of small apes at their place of murder" (90). Later yet, "children tottering and blinking in the pistolfire" (174) meet their untimely death during the massacre of the Tiguas. The most horrifying aspect of these moments is their dispassionate narration, which is as paratactic as the landscape description and semantically undifferentiated from the latter. In one episode, the gang's Delaware trackers become murderers of Apache infants when "one of the Delawares emerged from the smoke with a naked infant dangling in each hand and squatted at a ring of midden stones and swung them by the heels each in turn and bashed their heads against the stones so that the brains burst forth through the fontanel in a bloody spew" (156).[18] There is ample evidence that infancy is used as a theme to evoke the mindless violence of self-abjection, imagined by the narrative consciousness and channeled through the kid. This quintessential function of the child imagery is moreover suggested by the use of the present tense for the novel's overture (containing the line "See the child") and its conclusion (containing the phrase "like an enormous infant"), whereas the past tense is used throughout the bulk of the text.

The significance of the child iconography is further insinuated in descriptions of the judge. While children expire in his hands, the judge himself resembles a demonic child revenant. Roughly a page after the "child" is "finally divested of all that he has been" (4) and metamorphoses into "the kid" (5), Judge Holden is introduced as looking "strangely childlike" (6). Time and again, the judge's infantile or fetal features are alluded to by references to his baldness, hairlessness, paleness, smallness of extremities, or nudity. He appears "outsized and childlike with his naked face" (79) and with "oddly childish lips" (140). The very sentence likening the judge to "an enormous infant" because he has "small feet," and is "naked," "pale and hairless," concedes that he is "[t]owering" and "huge" (335). His height is given as "close on to seven feet" (6), his weight as "twenty-four stone" (128) or 336 pounds: "an enormous infant" indeed. The grotesqueness of this albino figure is enhanced as the narrative turns him into something like the Antichrist with a Nietzschean rhetoric; a confidence man of altering appearance who appears anywhere, anytime; a conjurer adept at tricks; a master of ceremonies at many a dance; a walking encyclopedia.

In effect, the oxymoronic picture of the "enormous infant" suggests that the judge monopolizes the child motif as a figurative representation of the subconscious (the "real" in Lacan's terminology) that Kristeva defines as "not an Object but the Thing. Let me posit the 'Thing' as the real that does not lend itself to signification" (*Sun* 13). The monstrous child emerges as an emblem of that abject "Thing" inducing the type of melancholy psychosis that seems to afflict the kid in *Blood Meridian*. It functions as an aesthetic motif more than as a psychological symptom, and its meaning is the death wish of the subject.

The fact that the familiar aphorism of pastoral nostalgia, "*et in Arcadia ego*" (125),[19] is set into Judge Holden's rifle stock suggests that death—an incidental fact of existence in traditional pastoralism—has become the formative experience of wilderness pastoralism. The novel's third epigraph on the scalped skull that is three hundred thousand years old says as much, insinuating that the earth has been a place of mayhem since time immemorial. The discussion of McCarthy's work so far should make it easy to see why the judge is constructed as an allegorical agent much like the satanic leader of the triune in *Outer Dark*. While the kid directs the narrative gaze and—like Culla in *Outer Dark*—represents the narrative melancholia over a world gone to ruin, the judge represents a figure of death, Thanatos incarnate. The fact that this typological role is projected through the eyes of the kid but continues to be projected after the kid's death, identifies the Thanatos as the prime mover of the kid's and the narrator's psyches alike. The kid's dreams of the judge are among the few insights into his mind. As with Lester's dreams in *Child of God*, the language of the dreams is too sophisticated to be the kid's. It is the narrator who projects, more than he relates, the kid's nightmares as parables about the judge, representing him as the personified void of prenatal and posthumous existence:

> In that sleep and in sleeps to follow the judge did visit. Who would come other? A great shambling mutant, silent and serene. Whatever his antecedents he was something wholly other than their sum, nor was there system by which to divide him back into his origins for he would not go. Whoever would seek out his history through what unraveling of loins and ledgerbooks must stand at last darkened and dumb at the shore of a void without terminus or origin and whatever science he might bring to bear upon the dusty primal matter blowing down out of the millennia will discover no trace of any ultimate atavistic egg by which to reckon his commencing. (309–10)

Since the typology of the judge ultimately refers to death itself, the inscription on his rifle could not be more appropriate. Who else but Death would celebrate war as the ultimate game of chance because it determines the personal or collective aptitude for survival?

This angle on the judge makes instant sense of his glorification of war. Not only is war eternal and sacred, the judge claims in sinister perversion of the comic way, but in a world of total anarchy, war is the only thing that is sacred: "War is the ultimate game because war is at last a forcing of the unity of existence. War is god" (249). This tirade, inspired by the congenial environment of the desert, turns terrorism into dogma. Its essence is reemphasized when the judge virtually identifies himself as the grim reaper: "What do you think death is, man? Of whom do we speak when we speak of a man who was and is not? Are these blind riddles or are they not some part of every man's jurisdiction? What is death if not an agency? And whom does he intend toward" (329)? The judge's allegorical agency as Death is further suggested when he answers, "You speak truer than you know" to the kid's disclaimer, "You aint nothin," and when he identifies Death as the lead dancer by asking "there will be one there always who is a true dancer and can you guess who that might be" (331)?

Unsurprisingly, the entire episode at the Beehive Saloon is confabulated into a parable on the dance of death. The location represents in grotesque microcosm a civilization in decline, while the kid's murder becomes a sacrificial ritual. The episode's macabre atmosphere is created in part through explicit and implicit intertextuality with European literature, such as the reference to Mignon in Goethe's *Wilhelm Meister* in the figures of the organ-grinding girl and the showman "in a tyrolean costume" (324), and the subchapter heading altering a line from *Tonio Kröger* into "Sie müssen schlafen aber Ich muss tanzen" (316).[20] Even more poignantly, the following scene evokes medieval images of mankind supine before Death or assembled for Judgment Day: "He [the judge] wore a round hat with a narrow brim and he was among every kind of man, herder and bullwhacker and drover and freighter and miner and hunter and soldier and pedlar and gambler and drifter and drunkard and thief and he was among the dregs of the earth in beggary a thousand years and he was among the scapegrace scions of eastern dynasties and in all that motley assemblage he sat by them and yet alone as if he were some other sort of man entire and he seemed little changed or none in all these years" (325). Four pages later the novel proper ends with the familiar emblem of the judge dancing into self-proclaimed immortality ("He *says* that he will never die" [emphasis added]). How much clearer—short of titling the image "Dancing Death"—could an allegory on death be? Thus the novel ends in a powerful incantation of Death triumphant, narrated in the calculated parataxis of a fugue. This concluding emblem of the judge as "a bloated angel of war and death" (Pilkington 317), is followed by a strange epilogue allegorizing the mindless westward progress of civilization. The epilogue is ecocritical only in the most apocalyptic sense, as if the prevalence of death were to define once again McCarthy's wilderness pastoralism.

In this sense, the initial question as to "whether the stuff of creation may be shaped to man's will or whether his own heart is not another kind of clay" (5) is ultimately moot. Even as both ends of the opposition—the hubris of humankind versus human implication in physical materiality—are horribly enacted in the novel's terrorism and thereby prove their validity: They are both subject to the erasure of death. One of the subchapter headings of chapter 7 is "Tertium quid" (81), designating an intermediate factor that defies classification into either of two groups. In the light of the evidence, this third factor is not the comic way of survival—as it should be in a picaresque or ecopastoral novel—but death. The tertium quid implied in the subchapter in question is the negative essence of death: "[T]he ragged flames fled down the wind as if sucked by some maelstrom out there in the void, some vortex in that waste apposite to which man's transit and his reckonings alike lay abrogate. As if beyond will or fate he and his beasts and his trappings moved both in card and in substance under consignment to some third or other destiny" (96). Various essential passages continue the theme of a third factor of existence, suggesting its supremacy over the dichotomy in opposition to which it defines itself. Some of the most enigmatic passages become deeply meaningful in their reference to this third agency, such as the judge's observation that "in this was expressed the very nature of the witness and that his proximity was no third thing but rather the prime" (153), or the description of shadows as "rearing with a terrible redundancy behind them like some third aspect of their presence hammered out black and wild upon the naked grounds" (151–52). An old Mexican speaks of death as a "another caballero and I think that no man hides from him" (103).[21] Moreover, in the novel's predominant setting, the desert, "death seemed the most prevalent feature of the landscape" (48). Vice versa, desert is the place where the judge, Death incarnate, originates (125).

Thus, while idealizing the coexistential aspect of optical democracy, the novel emphasizes human complicity with the desert's lethal indifference. Small wonder that the final chapter contains a plaintive account of a man-made ecological disaster, the extermination of the buffalo: "They're gone. Ever one of them that God ever made is gone as if they'd never been at all" (316–17). The apocalyptic nature of human progress is evoked in the frontier allegory of the epilogue and prefigured in the hermit's misanthropic jeremiad (19). In effect, the narrative consciousness seems reconciled to the *negatively* egalitarian paradigm of a moribund frontier world in which man and nature struggle side by side for survival and lose the struggle to the merciless conditions on the desert's blood meridian. The ecopastoral gist of *Blood Meridian,* then, is that the terms of biocentrism are dictated by the fact of death, more than by ecological interdependence. Instead of a progressive ecopastoralism, *Blood Meridian* offers a post-humanist variation of the baroque *vanitas* pastoralism.

The most consistent and affirmative message to be conveyed by both the historical and pastoral aspects of the novel may indeed be formulated in the judge's Social Darwinist sermons. These fail to differentiate between human ferocity and natural wildness, as the narrative voice fails to differentiate between extreme anthropocentrism and radical biocentrism. As outrageously fascist as this line of thought is, it reflects the fatalistic reaction of a narrative consciousness perceiving a final synthesis of all humanist dialectics in death. Caught between a residual humanism and emergent biocentrism, the narrator inhabits a limbo radically different from the animistic meta-discourse of *The Orchard Keeper* or the Border Trilogy. The same combination of ecocentric awareness and egocentric anguish informs the judge's belief that "there were no men anywhere in the universe save those upon the earth"[22] and that human stewardship over the earth is merely an illusion: "Even in this world more things exist without our knowledge than with it and the order in creation which you see is that which you have put there, like a string in a maze, so that you shall not lose your way. For existence has its own order and that no man's mind can compass, that mind itself being but a fact among others" (245). The post-humanist drift of this argument underlines the allegorical quality of the novel, for even as these ideas are verbalized by the judge—icon of Death and warlord—they ground themselves in the ecopastoral intention of the meta-narrative.

Ultimately, the judge's totalitarian claim merely represents an apocalyptic consummation of the biblical mission to "be fruitful and multiply, and replenish the earth, and subdue it: and have dominion over the fish of the sea, and over the fowl of the air, and over every living thing that moveth upon the earth" (Gen. 1:28). From a biocentric point of view, the idea that humans—sitting atop the food chain and being the most predatory of creatures—have stewardship over the world is at once deterministically cogent, and totalitarian. Accordingly, the novel's sense of evil manifests itself less in the genocidal campaigns of the scalp hunters than in the mindless extermination of the buffalo, the greed-inspired migration of "[I]tinerant degenerates bleeding westward like some heliotropic plague" (78), and the man-made, machine-driven "evil that can run itself a thousand years" (19). This evil is described in the epilogue's scenario of the "wanderers in search of bones and those who do not search and they move haltingly in the light like mechanisms whose movements are monitored with escapement and pallet so that they appear restrained by a prudence or reflectiveness which has no inner reality" (337).

Although *Blood Meridian* is committed to an egalitarian aesthetic of "optical democracy," the absolute indifference of the natural environment and the absolute license of the social environment combine in the text as if to subject picaresque survivalism and relational biocentrism jointly to the universal truth of entropy and death. Arguably then, *Blood Meridian* ought to be read as not just a revisionist Western, nor as just an ecocritical Western, but as a historicist epos in the sense that it negotiates the meaning of human history—like *Moby Dick*—within a meaningful nature, and thereby qualifies its existential status. The wildness and vastness of the ocean there, desert here, identify death as the sole arbiter in the struggle between human will and the materiality of nature, a tertium quid personified by the weaver god (446) in *Moby Dick* and—in addition to the judge—by the "pale sutler" (44) in *Blood Meridian*. Apart from the biocentric survivalism of the wilderness, the novel ventures no ethical or historiographic tenets.

Thus it is in a very negative sense that *Blood Meridian* stylizes frontier history into an egalitarian "natural history" of man in nature (*see* Phillips, "History" 443), and yet its effect on the reader is a positive, therapeutic one. The insistence on articulation—turning the enigma of sorrow into the ambiguous emblem of the "monstrous child"—induces a strange euphoria, both in the melancholy narrator crafting the emblem and in the reader susceptible to its meaning. Kristeva contends that allegory "endows the lost signifier with a signifying pleasure, a resurrectional jubilation even to the stone and corpse, by asserting itself as coextensive with the subjective experience of a named melancholia—of melancholy jouissance" (*Sun* 102). Shaviro seems to read *Blood Meridian* along the same lines when suggesting, "Bloody death is our monotonously predictable destiny; yet its baroque opulence is attended with a frighteningly complicitous joy" (146). "See the child," the novel invites the reader; and in the light of Shaviro's "complicitous joy," this becomes an invitation to balance pastoral melancholia (over the fact that everything is equally worthless) with ecopastoral elation (over the fact that everything has equal value).

CHAPTER THREE

"Some Site Where Life Had Not Succeeded"

Ecopastoralism in the Border Trilogy

> Man has built up the rational world by his own efforts, but there remains within him an undercurrent of violence. Nature herself is violent, and however reasonable we may grow we may be mastered anew by a violence no longer that of nature but that of a rational being who tries to obey but who succumbs to stirrings within himself which he cannot bring to heel.
>
> Georges Bataille, *Erotism*

The pastoralism of Cormac McCarthy's Border Trilogy constitutes these novels' most overlooked aspect, and this not despite their relative accessibility, but because of it. The simplicity of the quest stories, the generic proximity to the Western, and the conventionality of the plot structures as heroic journeys have apparently caused the novels' complexity to go largely unacknowledged. Interpretations that confine themselves to the realistic surfaces of *All the Pretty Horses, The Crossing,* and *Cities of the Plain* do not necessarily constitute misreadings, yet they ignore the novels' multiple layers and their ecopastoral essence. More than the wilderness pastoralism of the preceding novels, the Border Trilogy undertakes a positive definition of McCarthy's ecopastoralism. The redefined meaning of pastoral manifests itself even on the plot level, as a look at the stories of the three novels will illustrate.

All the Pretty Horses (1992) contrasts starkly with the endemic depravity of *Blood Meridian,* while returning to the same Southwestern/Mexican setting. The novel's rather tame story, its conventional plot structure, and its seemingly realistic narration have prompted Gail Morrison to suggest, "*All the Pretty Horses* is set in a world of comparative normalcy" (177). Morrison identifies three plotlines in *All the Pretty Horses:* John Grady's "doomed romance" with the hacendado's daughter, Alejandra Rocha; the "marvelously detailed business of horse herding, breaking and breeding"; and "the Jimmy Blevins subplot" (181). The novel's setting is specific and realistic, being

> firmly grounded in the details of time (1949–1951) and place (west Texas in and around San Angelo, southeast to San Antonio, southwest to Langtrey and Pumpville,

> farther south to various locations in the Mexican border state of Coahuila, and farther south still to Zachatechas), and topography (mountains, mesas, marshes, deserts, rivers). And like its immediate predecessor, *All the Pretty Horses* is infused with the tensions of conflicting and competing cultures (the Anglo, the Comanche, the mestizo, the Mexican, the Spaniard) and economies (the agrarian-pastoral and the industrial-commercial, the legal and the illegal). (Morrison 175)

Parts 1 and 4 of the novel are devoted to the journeys into and out of Mexico, while part 2 covers the incidents at the hacienda, La Purísima, and part 3 covers those in prison. Deaths in the family mark the novel's beginning and end, causing John Grady to cross the border into Mexico both times. Morrison, among others, suggests that the plot of *All the Pretty Horses* is structured like a pastoral initiation tale: "For this novel is fundamentally a *Bildungsroman,* a coming of age story in the great tradition of Hawthorne, Twain, Melville, and James, that archetypal American genre in which a youthful protagonist turns his back on civilization and heads out—into the forest, down river, across the sea or, as in John Grady's case, through desert and mountain on horseback—into the wilderness where innocence experiences the evil of the universe and risks defeat by it" (178). After the quest fails, initiating the boys primarily into the reality of death and loss, the novel ends with John Grady's crossing "into the darkening land, the world to come" (302). More so than the two subsequent volumes of the trilogy, *All the Pretty Horses* tries to visualize an eco-pastoral alternative to the anthropocentric land management left behind in Texas, and it identifies it, for a time, in the protagonists' life and horsemanship at Don Héctor's hacienda.

The Crossing (1994)—almost identical in setting, structure, and mood—presents a Western-like narrative generically close to *All the Pretty Horses* but thematically more akin to the mystical pastoralism of McCarthy's early work. The plot and figures of this second volume of the Border Trilogy do not continue the story of volume 1, launching instead a new cast of characters and a new plotline. Moreover, the novel is set in the immediate prewar period and in the wake of a long and miserably failed revolution in Mexico, that is, about a decade earlier than the time frame of *All the*

Pretty Horses. Once again, the story begins just north of the border, in the boot heel of New Mexico, and Billy Parham, the protagonist, is sixteen years old, the same age as John Grady Cole.

Billy grows up on a small cattle ranch. Watching a pack of wolves hunt in the moonlight becomes a formative childhood experience for him. Later on, the wolves reappear in a dream "as if they burned with some inner fire and the wolves twisted and turned and leapt in a silence such that they seemed of another world entire" (4).[1] One winter a lone female wolf starts preying on the livestock. Although the last known trapper has—significantly—vanished along with his woodcraft wisdom, Billy, his brother Boyd, and their father attempt to trap the animal. When Billy finally captures the she-wolf, he decides (inspired by his dreams and the presence of a trespassing Native American) to repatriate her to the wilderness across the border. Thus commences the first of three crossings into another country, not to mention Billy's crossing into the feudal order of an older time and into manhood. The nature of the three quest journeys seems melodramatic and contrived in summary, but the novel's essence manifests itself yet again in its overwhelming use of allegory, what with the lengthy parables of the heretic, the blind veteran, and the Gitano. Ultimately, the novel as a whole becomes a fable on the genesis of a relational sense of self rather than on an ecopastoral utopia.

On the plot level, Billy's irresponsible and quixotic enterprise[2] predictably ends in disaster when the wolf is first quarantined in Mexico, then exhibited as a carnival act, and finally baited in a pit fight with dogs. Upon his return home Billy finds the paternal ranch deserted, for his parents have been murdered in their sleep, defenseless without the rifle he carried off on his wilderness expedition. Since the crime seems to have been committed by Native Americans (or so the sheriff suspects) the succor Billy denied earlier to a vaguely sinister Native American[3] perhaps foreshadows both the murders and the theme of hospitality that plays a central role in the novel. The novel fails to elaborate how Billy comes to terms with the loss, while being very explicit about the trauma of Boyd, who has survived and is staying with neighbors. Almost without hiatus the plot resumes, reporting Billy's reunion with Boyd, their ill-planned departure for Mexico to recover the six horses stolen from their ranch, their theft of one of the horses, their rescue of a solitary girl from impending rape, the seizure of three more of the horses, Boyd's injury by the pursuers, and eventually Boyd's elopement with the girl they rescued. This second part of *The Crossing* contains mysterious encounters with friendly strangers and a commedia dell'arte troupe. Epiphanic moments of kindness and hospitality contrast with the awful machinery of vengeance set in motion by the abduction of the horses. Suffering from loneliness after Boyd's defection, Billy crosses back into the United States toward the end of 1943, ignorant of the fact that the country is at war.

Billy's third journey, finally, is undertaken after unsuccessful attempts to enlist in the army in spite of a heart condition. His aimless drifting in search of his brother takes him deeper into Mexico, until he eventually arrives at Boyd's grave. Although consistently denying him the boon he sets out for, Billy's third quest completes the two earlier ones insofar as he restores Boyd—rather than the wolf—to his native soil, and recovers his patrimony more in the form of Boyd's remains than in the form of the horses. After a moment of absolute despondency during which Billy finds himself in a deserted shack by the highway and witnesses the first atomic blast in history, the novel ends on an epiphanic note: "He took off his hat and placed it on the tarmac before him and he bowed his head and held his face in his hands and wept. He sat there for a long time and after a while the east did gray and after a while the right and godmade sun did rise, once again, for all and without distinction" (425–26).[4] The novel's main structural difference from both *All the Pretty Horses* and *Cities of the Plain* is that it goes further in creating a fable-like cosmos at odds with any authentic location, and despite all realistic detail. It stylizes Mexico into an ecopastoral idyll removed from a civilization at war and from desert desolation. Its distinguishing feature is that it is not the United States, perhaps because American pastoralism needs "as the century ends, an older and darker Arcadia in which to be enacted" (Hass 41).

Cities of the Plain (1998), the third volume of the Border Trilogy,[5] is caught between the idea of Mexico as an ecopastoral utopia and the treacherous reality of the Mexican border town of Juarez. Confusing the two, John Grady loses his life in his ill-fated courtship of Magdalena, a teenage prostitute and epileptic. While it returns superficially to the realistic narration and simplistic plot progression of *All the Pretty Horses*, *Cities of the Plain* reveals its meaning on an allegorical level that attains the autonomy of a parable in the epilogue. Within the trilogy, *Cities of the Plain* is the aesthetically weakest volume, marked by false pathos and nostalgia. Regarding the pastoral aspect retarded by the foregrounded sinfulness of the cities of the plain,[6] Arnold writes that it "is a diminished world that McCarthy creates in *Cities of the Plain,* a postwar West suffering through its final mockeries and subtractions, a world hard pressed for heroics and depending instead on simple decency. Neither John Grady nor Billy has been spared these diminishments" ("First Look" 222). Nor has the natural world been spared such diminishment, for the pastoral dream of cowboy romanticism is contested here by the military's acquisition of rangeland. What remains of the ecopastoral vision in this final volume of the trilogy comes close to pastoral nostalgia of the most conventional kind, even if couched in a new setting, and neither the parabolic dream sequence of the epilogue nor the dedication at the end of the book succeed in elevating this melodrama to the level of McCarthy's first five novels.

Cities of the Plain brings the protagonists of the first two volumes together as fellow cowboys on the ranch of one Mac McGovern near Alamogordo, New Mexico, and not far from El Paso, Texas. Billy—nine years older than John Grady—has taken on the role of an avuncular friend who tries to keep John Grady out of the romantic trouble for which he shows such affinity. More so than John Grady, Billy has metamorphosed from a melancholy nomad into a kindhearted skeptic, thoroughly weaned from his teenage wolf-mysticism, whereas John Grady's teenage traits of solipsism and romantic delusion (both as to women and horsemanship) have hardened into melancholy obsessions. His adversary, the pimp Eduardo, correctly diagnoses John Grady's spiritual malady in his conversation with Billy, arguing, "The world may be many different ways for them but there is one world that will never be and that is the world they dream of" (134). This is one level of the truth, but a more dire truth is that Eduardo himself is in love with Magdalena and that both suitors are about to die in their back-alley duel after Tiburcio, Eduardo's henchman, has murdered Magdalena during her escape. Arnold writes that the novel "is primarily a story of male friendship, such as, in fact, are found throughout McCarthy's writings" ("First Look" 237), and the same is suggested by the parable of the padrino told by the Tiresias figure of the blind maestro (192–96). But in a lot of ways the novel is as much about grief and the work of memory as are the other two volumes of the trilogy.

The novel's epilogue consists primarily of Billy, now seventy-eight years old, discussing death with another nomadic figure, a Mexican vagrant. The conversation resembles the classic pastoral eclogue, but it hardly articulates anything not already suggested in the earlier novels. Unfortunately for the ecopastoral critic, the epilogue also contains two instances of demystification that deny the narrative thrust of McCarthy's work. Sitting "by the highwayside" at night, Billy beholds a structure "he took for one of the ancient Spanish missions of that country but when he studied it again he saw that it was the round white domes of a radar tracking station." He also sees "a row of figures" resembling perhaps the penitents in *Blood Meridian* (313–14) but which turn out to be "only rags of plastic wrapping hanging from a fence where the wind had blown them" (289). This unexpected insistence on a purely gnostic reality defuses the very workings of allegoresis that have served as principal carrier of pastoral meaning in McCarthy's work. It suggests the datedness of pastoralism in itself even as the trilogy continues to discuss it. Perhaps then it is in regard to the pastoral as to other aspects that the dedication at the end of *Cities of the Plain* states: "The story's told" (293).

The present argument can draw on mimetic readings of these novels for certain formal aspects that have parallels in McCarthy's previous works. All three of the novels are open-ended, episodic narratives told by an unidentified narrator whose point of view rests throughout with protagonists John Grady Cole and Billy Parham, respectively (except for subchapters in *Cities of the Plain* where Magdalena provides the point of view). *All the Pretty Horses* and *The Crossing* are structured as picaresque initiation quests. The genre of the Western is modified in *All the Pretty Horses* and *The Crossing* into tales of inverted frontier life, the frontier being neither the outpost of civilization in a howling wilderness nor a desolate purgatory as in *Blood Meridian*, but a last pastoral stronghold against civilization. The mythological themes dramatized include mainstays of McCarthy's fictional universe, such as the dispossessed yeoman and Jeffersonian agrarianism, the last cowboy and the frontier, the New Adam and rugged individualism.

These observations may be found in any mimetic reading of *All the Pretty Horses,* and this in spite of the fact that the presence of myths and picaresque figures signals, not mimetic but stylized, multilevel writing.[7] Among these signals—indicating the existence of a meta-narrative—are certain less-than-realistic elements, which neither the plot progression nor the story proper call for, and which run the danger of rendering these tales melodramatic. Why, for instance, are the tales of Dueña Alfonsa interpolated at great length in *All the Pretty Horses;* why are the tales of the Mormon, the blind veteran, and the Gitano interpolated in *The Crossing;* and those of old Mr. Johnson, the blind maestro, and the vagrant in *Cities of the Plain?* Why do the novels refer the reader time and again to the sadness of other characters, such as Alejandra, John Grady's father, Boyd, Magdalena, Mac, and Socorro? And why do they, from the start, immerse John Grady and Billy—at least in the trilogy's first two novels—in a despondency that is disproportional and untypical for young picaresque heroes and that exceeds its function as an element of romance? Why make the denouement of their stories (returning to the United States from Mexico) anticlimactic, when the texts have prepared for a happy ending (justice at home)? Why does John Grady's melancholia persist even in the face of auspicious prospects, and bring about his death? Finally, why does Billy choose a nomadic, ascetic lifestyle over the recovery of his inheritance or a settled life in both *The Crossing* and *Cities of the Plain?*

Along with these inconsistencies, other aspects and the paratactic narrative rhythm refer us to the structural complexities of the novel. Some hesitancy to define the deeper level of meaning in *All the Pretty Horses* seems to linger despite a certain consensus among critics that it exists. Nancy Kreml shows how the author "establishes a transparent style, with little limitation of interpretation, against which he plays a secondary, more highly constrained foregrounded style; further, he uses the elements of the foregrounded style to signal a thematic shift, an intrusion of another level of meaning" (Kreml 138). Having identified this discursive striation and catalogued its specificities, however, Kreml neglects to draw certain conclusions that her inquiry encourages. What makes her observation important is that the discursive striation of allegoresis constitutes a familiar hallmark of McCarthy's prose.

Allegorical discourse is structured by the dialogic tension between a parabolic surface meaning and ulterior levels of meaning.

That the story of *All the Pretty Horses* remains perfectly intelligible even if the secondary, allegorical layer is ignored must be considered the secret of the novel's success, because many readers have taken *All the Pretty Horses* for little more than an unconventional Western. The option of restricting oneself to a superficial reading of the romantic yarn, oblivious to the correlated layers of allegorical meaning, is clearly not as available to readers of *Outer Dark*. This would explain both why *Outer Dark* did *not* sell half a million copies and why McCarthy was uneasy about the fact that *All the Pretty Horses* did.[8]

As said above, these novels try to redefine literary pastoralism along not just pessimistically post-humanist but optimistically ecopastoral lines. Although all three novels are pastoral tales in their own right, they form, taken together, an overarching structure composed of the three pastoral motifs defined by Marx (escape into the pastoral realm, immersion into pastoral harmony, and return to urban civilization). The pastoralism prevalent in the trilogy disagrees with McCarthy's own literary convention insofar as wilderness has already been established by *Blood Meridian*—and to a lesser degree by *Child of God*—as the ideal pastoral space. Rather than mourning the demise of Arcadian nature, the trilogy's narrative voice directs its pastoral nostalgia toward a lifestyle closely associated with the Southwestern wilderness. Nonetheless, this lifestyle is as anachronistic as that of the traditional pastoral realm, even as it modifies traditional pastoralism into an egalitarian commitment to the materiality of both nature (pastoral landscape) and discourse (storytelling). The survivalist thrust—emerging prominently in *Blood Meridian*—defies the narrative melancholia and embraces an affirmative ecopastoralism on the brink of disintegration.

As discussed in the chapter on *Outer Dark*, allegory and melancholia complement each other. Once again, melancholia and allegory work in sync in the Border Trilogy, one functioning as narrative mood, the other as a literary device for articulating it. Assuming that something like a "melancholy gaze"[9] characterizes the perceptual mode that induces allegoresis, one can start identifying the melancholia underlying the texts.

The first of the novels, *All the Pretty Horses* commences with the wake for John Grady's late grandfather, the opening pages introducing all three of the aesthetic elements listed above (pastoral, allegorical, and melancholic): There is the death-centered gaze in John Grady's words at the deathbed: "That was not sleeping. That was not sleeping" (3); there is a moment of pastoral crisis in the invasion of the rural setting by the train that John Grady watches approach "boring out of the east like some ribald satellite of the coming sun" (3); there is a *vanitas* motif in his outdoor meditation "like a man come to the end of something" (5) and a *memento mori* motif in his contemplation of "an old horseskull" (6). Steeping the text in sadness from its very first lines, these stock emblems of pastoral allegoresis are offered before the real trouble has even started, and a portentous opening they make.

By the end of the trilogy's first novel there will have been sorrow enough to go around. John Grady will have lost the ranch; his father; his lover, Alejandra; and his substitute mother, Abuela. He will find himself estranged from his mother; his former girlfriend; his friend Rawlins; and Don Héctor, the one employer who put faith in him. He will have witnessed Blevins being killed, and he will have killed a man himself. *The Crossing,* the novel's sequel, continues in this vein because Billy loses, in turn, both of his parents, his brother, their patrimony (the horses), and the hope to reintegrate himself into mainstream American life (through his failure to enlist in the Army and his failure to return to the parental homestead). At the end of *Cities of the Plain,* John Grady will have lost his wife-to-be, and his very life to their suicidal romance; Billy will have been reduced to an introverted drifter. Despite the melodramatic hardships on the plot level, however, the melancholia felt by the protagonists actually seems to precede these hardships and contribute to bringing them about through a sense of premonition, like a self-fulfilling prophecy. There is ample detail, plus the example of the foregoing novels, to suggest that the narrator's underlying melancholia is stylizing the narrative events into parables of fate.

The first novel's inventory of sorrow prompts Morrison to observe, "Like virtually all of McCarthy's work to date, *All the Pretty Horses* is permeated with a sense of loss, alienation, deracination and fragmentation" (175). Interestingly, these terms—loss, alienation, deracination, fragmentation—catalog the very sources of melancholia. As discussed in the previous chapters, the process of ego formation succumbs to melancholia if and when the abject subject fails to negate its loss via libidinal sublimation of the

Thanatos, and the loss expresses itself instead in endless mourning, in suicidal alienation, in social deracination, and in an obsession with images of fragmentation. When Dueña Alfonsa in *All the Pretty Horses* suggests, "Between the wish and the thing the world lies waiting" (238), she situates the melancholic's alienated existence between loss and the obsessive preoccupation with the restoration of the lost object.

But how could such a psychological profile be applicable to John Grady's character, or Billy's? Teenage boys would seem unlikely to set out on pastoral quests across the boundaries of country, culture, and age if they were caught up in a catatonic state of sorrow. What is more, John Grady and Billy, whose misfortunes may be exceptional, but are hardly atypical for either a picaresque novel or a Western, remain true picaros of the cowboy tradition—restless, resourceful, and independent—even after everything that *can* take a turn for the worse has. Still, evidence for a melancholy state of mind surfaces on the first pages of the first novel. The problem at the bottom of the trilogy's melancholia is summed up in the statement that John Grady "felt wholly alien to the world although he loved it still" (*Horses* 282). This passage goes on to expand John Grady's grief (over having lost Alejandra) into an allegory of the melancholic's dilemma of being caught between the compulsive contemplation of death and a simultaneous attachment to the material world. Some instances reflecting on the protagonists' alienation read like the clinical symptoms of melancholia, such as the following excerpts, one for each of the trilogy's volumes:

> He thought that in the beauty of the world were hid a secret. He thought the world's heart beat at some terrible cost and that the world's pain and its beauty moved in a relationship of diverging equity and that in this headlong deficit the blood of multitudes might ultimately be exacted for the vision of a single flower. (*Horses* 282)

> He lifted his face and stood by the roadside and his thoughts were that other than wind and rain nothing would ever come again to touch him out of that estrangement that was the world. Not in love, not in enmity. The bonds that fixed him in the world had become rigid. Where he moved the world moved also and he could never

> approach it and he could never escape it. He sat in the roadside weeds in the rain and wept. (*Crossing* 279)
>
> When he rode into the yard it was raining lightly and he could see them all at supper through the rainbleared glass of the kitchen window. . . . He thought it was like seeing these people in some other time before he'd ever come to the ranch. Or they were like people in some other house of whose lives and histories he knew nothing. Mostly they all just seemed to be waiting for things to be a way they'd never be again. (*Cities* 233–34)

Once again, the meditations ascribed to the protagonists' point of view in these quotes are clad in rhetoric beyond their intellectual scope (phrases like "diverging equity").

If nothing else, this observation suggests the discrepancy between the sober chronicling of dynamic action and the somber recording of static thought. Although the surface discourse is disinterested enough to give a plausible account of John Grady's or Billy's outer progress, the true commitment of the narrative is obviously to the nonmimetic meta-discourse on their inner state. In fact, the plot progression seems to be principally motivated by the desire to position the contents of the secondary discursive strain that is inherently melancholy, allegorical, and therefore neither mimetic nor disinterested. So while it is safe to say that John Grady's and Billy's alienation is captured in the meta-narrative, it is even more appropriate to say inversely that the melancholia of the meta-narrative—which is the narrator's—couches itself in the allegorical enactment of the boys' alienated existence.

Among the various passages in *All the Pretty Horses* that combine melancholy mood with allegorical mode, the following instance reads virtually like a classic *vanitas* image: "He slept that night in a field far from any town. He built no fire. He lay listening to the horse crop the grass at his stakerope and he listened to the wind in the emptiness and watched stars trace the arc of the hemisphere and die in the darkness at the edge of the world and as he lay there the agony in his heart was like a stake" (256). Instances such as this one, while containing enough personal sorrow to account for the textual melancholia, bespeak a rhetorical excess in their reiteration of sorrow that transcends the protagonist's personal biography and identifies its events as allegorical tales of fate. The foregoing conclusion that the protagonists' portraiture is compromised by their infusion with the melancholia of the meta-narrative is corroborated by the text's inclusion of other saturnine figures beside them, such as John Grady's father, Alejandra, and Dueña Alfonsa in *All the Pretty Horses,* and Boyd, the hermit, the blind man, and the Gitano in *The Crossing,* and Magdalena, Mac, old Mr. Johnson, and Socorro in *Cities of the Plain.*

Moreover, recurrent emblems of pastoral loss that occur independently of the protagonists' sorrow suggest the meta-narrative melancholia. One of these emblems, in *All the Pretty Horses,* is John Grady's vision of the Comanches, "nation and ghost of nation passing in a soft chorale across that mineral waste to darkness bearing lost to all history and remembrance like a grail the sum of their secular and transitory and violent lives" (5). Despite the tragic aspect of the image, one ought to bear in mind that these Comanches are in fact the revenants of the "legion of horribles" wiping out Captain White's mercenaries in *Blood Meridian* (52). Even within the context of the grief on the plot level this ecopastoral twilight of the gods seems hyperbolic, and it would make the texts appear hopelessly melodramatic were it read in any way other than allegorically.

As seen in the chapters on *Outer Dark* and *Blood Meridian,* allegories—while evoking the presence of anterior allegories by reiterating their absence—always also signify ultimate absence, the nothingness or void of death itself. Kristeva's praise of allegory "as lavishness of that which *no longer is,* but which regains for myself a higher meaning because I am able to remake nothingness" (*Sun* 99) captures an essential aspect of allegoresis. The surplus meaning of allegory, its semantic excess, renders it capable of expressing ineffable meaning, such as the meaning of loss as such. Allegory's negative aspect of continuously deferring meaning to typological antecedents is compensated by the automatic ordering of these references into sequence. While reiterating his internal predicament, the melancholic's allegorical discourse always also aligns the external world and its history with his melancholy gaze, which in an act of discursive self-empowerment subordinates the outer macrocosm to the inner microcosm of his stunted self. As a case in point, Billy perceives his own biography in a moment of dejection quasi-posthumously, as a tale already told: "He seemed to himself a person with no prior life. As if he had died in some way years ago and was ever after some other being who had no history, who had no ponderable life to come" (*Crossing* 382). At the price of being dead to this world, Billy assumes control over the story of his life and renders himself immune to the dangers of the present. His feeling that he is a relict from the past is confirmed by the reaction of people when he passes on horseback through the town of Deming, after returning from his second trip to Mexico: "The few cars that passed gave him all the berth that narrow road afforded and the people looked back at him through the rolling dust as if he were a thing wholly alien in that landscape. Something from an older time of which they'd only heard. Something of which they'd read" (*Crossing* 334). Similarly, John Grady's view of his own past after losing Alejandra becomes melancholy and selective: "He saw very clearly how all his life led only to this moment and all after led nowhere at all" (*Horses* 254). John Grady's observation harks back to the Dueña's notion of predestination and her consequent lack of "sympathy with people to whom things happen. It may be that their luck is bad, but is that to count in their favor?" (*Horses* 240). As will become clearer yet, the notion of fate—which is allegorical in its retrospective and prescriptive dynamics—is shared by characters, intratextual storytellers, and of course the narrative voice. The Dueña's view of history, for one, is subsumed under the narrative perspective and serves primarily to lend to the latter the authority of alleged historical truth (as it places the events of the main narrative in intertextual sequence with her account of history).

Benjamin suggests that storytelling treats personal biographies as well as history in a retrospective manner sanctioned by death, arguing that "a man . . . who died at thirty-five will appear to *remembrance* at every point of his life as the man who dies at the age of thirty-five" (*Illuminationen* 402). In fact, with its tales, parables, dreams, and general melancholia of things remembered, the trilogy seems to presuppose death as *the* semantic structuring principle.[10] Stories are grounded in the authority of death insofar as their dynamic remembrance is governed by a static perception of moments past. The agency of the story's subject is replaced by the agency of the storyteller so that only posthumously, commencing in the moment of death, a person's story takes on definitive shape: "When this moment has come, the corpse appears in the strangeness of its solitude as that which has disdainfully withdrawn from us. Then the feeling of a relation between humans is destroyed, and our mourning, the care we take of the dead and all the prerogatives of our former passions, since they can no longer know their direction, fall back upon us, return toward us. It is striking that at this very moment, when the cadaverous presence is the presence of the unknown before us, the mourned deceased begins to *resemble himself*" (Blanchot 257). The story resulting from such biographical remembrance suggests the determinism inherent in the notion of fate. Yet it is in fact the retrospection of such biographical remembrance that creates that very notion, because in retrospect the actions, consequences and reactions of a man's life do indeed arrogate the inevitability associated with predestination. In this sense, Judge Holden's assumption that "any man who could discover his own fate and elect therefore some opposite course could only come at last to that selfsame reckoning at the same appointed time" (*Blood Meridian* 330) actually represents a parable on the retrospective view of remembrance that inspires the idea of predestination. This retrospective logic at the bottom of the notion of fate manifests itself in *The Crossing* in a man's argument that "men believe death's elections to be inscrutable yet every act invites the act which follows and to the extent that men put one foot before the other they are accomplices in their own deaths as in all such facts of destiny" (379). Insofar as they—like dead bodies—resemble and simultaneously fail to resemble their subject, stories are inherently allegorical in their references to death and mortality. Even more so than stories, photographs—like those collected by the Gitano's father in *The Crossing*—remember people from the point of death *even if their deaths have not occurred yet*. In this sense, stories and photographs are allegories of the passage of time and of deaths foretold. The Gitano's conclusion of his anecdote on his father's collection of daguerreotypes supposes as much: "He said that what men do not understand is that what the dead have quit is itself no world but is also only the picture of the world in men's hearts" (*Crossing* 413). Seen as *memento mori* images, stories and pictures capture "the anterior future that the past bequeaths to the present" (Schleifer 330). This assumption regarding the nature of the narrator's retrospective allegorizing even of present events—and of his usurpation of the protagonist's point of view—is substantiated by the scene in which John Grady witnesses the photo session of a newlywed couple: "[T]hey stood on the steps for their photograph to be taken and in their antique formalwear posed there in front of the church they already had the look of old photos. In the sepia monochrome of a rainy day in that lost village they'd grown old instantly" (*Horses* 284). Clearly, the melancholia that perceives a newlywed couple as moribund emanates from the amorphous narrator, not John Grady, who even as he functions as perceptual medium cannot possibly testify to the "sepia monochrome" quality of the photos before they have even been printed. Having seen not the picture, but only the scene it records, John Grady cannot engage in such a nostalgic reflection, whereas the narrator's melancholy gaze translates the photographic *re*-presentation into a recollection of lives that *will have* passed, or have indeed passed, by the time he tells his tale.

Moreover, the photo scene indicates that not only the protagonist's perceptual autonomy is compromised by its subjection to the narrator's allegoresis but so is the overall representation of the material world and its history. The appropriation of John Grady's sorrowful state by the narrative point of view, and the persistence of his sorrows beyond the first novel's ending and up to his death in the third, indicate that the trilogy is not concerned with allegorizing personal grief alone, even if it does make John Grady—more than Billy—the principal vessel of it. Rather, the characters' melancholy tales read like pieces of an allegorical palimpsest that ultimately serves to place pastoral nostalgia in context with a melancholy view of history. This observation identifies an essential feature of allegory and is supported by Deborah Madsen's argument that "[a]llegorical repetition—the relationships among signs in a typological allegorical narrative—is a temporal process assuming difference as well as resemblance but denying the possibility of any complete identification. The language of allegory is then purely figurative; it is not based upon perception" (139). As a result of being placed in allegorical sequence, these very memories become depersonalized and generic. Thus, the legend of Boyd as retold in the "corrido" (the song that Billy keeps hearing throughout his third trip to Mexico) represents but a typological variation on the theme of the revolutionary hero: "It tells the tale of that solitary man who is all men" (*Crossing* 386). Projecting a static picture of history, "allegory superinduces a vertical or paradigmatic reading of correspondences upon a horizontal or syntagmatic chain of events" (Owens 208). To read reality and history alike as a chronicle of sequential events implies a shift away from a descriptive to a prescriptive mode of discourse. While being dramatized as spatial crossings between societies, John Grady's and Billy's quests resemble in effect journeys through time (from mid-twentieth-century, to ever more antiquated societal structures). The *vanitas* moments at the beginning of *All the Pretty Horses* (Native Americans, horse skull, John Grady's disproportional sorrow) seem incongruous less because they are out of place than because they are out of time. In the context of the allegorical concept of history they make perfect sense in their atemporal correspondence of past with present.

Unlike standard historiography that approaches the historical record with a plethora of models and methods, the allegorical chronicle fails to distinguish between history and myth. It perceives history not as an evolution spelled by cause and effect but as recurrent enactments of the drama whose individual events are highlighted as exemplary moments within the set course of history.[11] The chronicler makes it his task to place the course of history in line with a metaphysical truth because he considers history "essential only in the stages of its decay" (Benjamin, *Trauerspiel* 145). We find both of these concepts in the rival versions of the Rochas' family history in *All the Pretty Horses*. Don Héctor's account (144–46) is taking a historiographer's approach, whereas allegorical interpretation defines the Dueña's chronicling of history and its logic: "For me the world has always been more of a puppet show. But when one looks behind the curtain and traces the strings upward he finds they terminate in the hands of yet other puppets, themselves with their own strings which trace upward in turn, and so on. In my own life I saw these strings whose origins were endless enact the deaths of great men in violence and madness" (231). By structuring history as a ritual succession of stops and starts the allegorist's interpretation of history reflects his melancholy desire to read a metaphysical continuity into human existence that defies its transitory and discontinuous nature. In other words, "the insight into the transience of things, and the concern to rescue them for eternity, is one of the strongest motives in allegory" (Benjamin, *Trauerspiel* 199). For if allegory concerns itself with typological "projection—either spatial or temporal or both—of structure as sequence" (Owens 207), the allegorist can self-consciously employ it not only to highlight past and present according to his own memory, but also to force future events into line with that memory.

An example of such an arbitrarily imposed typology is given in the fatalism grounding the Dueña's father's "great sense of the connectedness of things" and the parable he uses to elaborate it: "He claimed that the responsibility for a decision could never be abandoned to a blind agency but could only be relegated to human decisions more and more remote from their consequences. The example he gave was of a tossed coin that was at one time a slug in a mint and of the coiner who took that slug from the tray and placed it in the die in one of two ways and from whose act all else followed, cara y cruz. No matter through whatever turnings nor how many of them. Till our turn comes at last and our turn passes" (*Horses* 230–31).[12] To the melancholy gaze, the past—yet another allegory—functions as a temporally removed preview of the present (which so becomes part of the past). In this sense the strange storyteller in *Cities of the Plain* suggests that "[t]he world of our fathers resides within us" (281), and that in the discursive ordering of the "events of the waking world" according to the internalized history of previous generations "[i]t is we who assemble them into the story which is us" (283). In its melancholy cosmology, allegorical storytelling is essentially catastrophic because it subjects to its retrospection even those deaths that have not yet occurred (the storyteller's and the listeners' own death). The storyteller, like the Mexican nomad in *Cities of the Plain,* suggests, "I have been here before. So have you. Everything is for the taking. Touch nothing" (288) out of respect for the way in which human memory negotiates between generations.

In this sense, it is the ritual impetus of storytelling that turns the discontinuity of human lives (temporality) into continuity (immortality) through the incremental (discontinuous) and spiral (continuous) rhythm of remembrance. Each generation passes on an updated version of the stories it inherited. Such generational remembering is exemplified in the collective memory of the Tarahumara (a truly pastoral, native culture): "The Tarahumara had watered here a thousand years and a good deal of what could be seen in the world had passed this way. Armored Spaniards and hunters and trappers and grandees and their women and slaves and fugitives and armies and revolutions and the dead and the dying. And all that was seen was told and all that was told remembered" (*Crossing* 192). Memory is preserved in the Tarahumara's case because theirs is an oral culture, given to storytelling. Proceeding in a cumulative rather than an ordering manner, the melancholy gaze of the allegorist translates historical progression into a ritual process. The vaqueros' tales "of the cattle and the horses and the young wild mares in their season and of a wedding in La Vega and a death at Víbora" (*Horses* 227)[13] are not inherently melancholy but are rendered melancholy by the implication of storyteller and audience as anticipated parts in the endless succession of tales (and by the paratactic structure of the sentence). They become reiterations of other, identical tales of what is forever incomplete, fragmentary, ruinous, and of human history subsumed under the natural history of life cycles.

That the trilogy's narrator does in fact perceive history as a chronicle of variations of parallel tales of sorrow is suggested by the regular interpolation of tales. The human lives represented are nothing more or less than discourse anthologized within the chronicle of a world that is itself allegorical. For "this world also which seems to us a thing of stone and flower and blood is not a thing at all but is a tale. And all in it is a tale and each tale the sum of all lesser tales and yet these also are the selfsame tale and contain as well all else within them. So everything is necessary. Every least thing" (*Crossing* 143). As outlined here, typological history signifies nothing so much as anteriority itself. In the pastoralism of the trilogy the nostalgia for anterior and lost pastoral origins becomes the vanishing point of its allegoresis and melancholia both: an imaginary wound that will not heal and keeps calling for rhetorical ointment. So the protagonists have to be read as allegorical figures, reenacting the old new tale of pastoral quest and failure.

The reason why loss itself ultimately functions as the sole referent of allegory in the trilogy is that other objects lost (beside the pastoral way of life) are mourned, such as lovers, family, friends, or animals. This general sense of loss is affirmed in old Mr. Johnson's answer to John Grady's question as to what the hardest lesson in life might be: "I dont know. Maybe it's just that when things are gone they're gone. They aint coming back" (*Cities* 126). The deep-seated sorrow articulating itself in words such as these suggests that, while the trilogy arranges old and new versions of pastoral in typological sequence to formulate an ecopastoralism more affirmative than the wilderness biocentrism of *Blood Meridian*, the narrative consciousness is given to melancholia here as there.

But what to make of this intricate structuring of the trilogy? Allegorical writing contains instructions for its own interpretation as well as the ideological parameter "attached to interpretation as a means of perceiving some ideal or absolute value manifest in an interpreted world" (Madsen 144). Predictably, the patent striation of the trilogy into narration of plot action on the one hand, and allegorical meta-narratives on the other, serves to situate a melancholia felt over the loss of pastoral vision, entirely in keeping with pastoral convention. What complicates the matter is that the trilogy simultaneously uses its allegorical structure to develop an ecopastoral alternative to traditional pastoralism. From Arthur Ownby's incarceration in *The Orchard Keeper,* to the foreclosure of Lester Ballard's farm in *Child of God,* to the protagonists' escapist endeavors in Mexico in the Border Trilogy, McCarthy's work has time and again addressed the datedness of the traditional pastoral vision even as it keeps invoking it. It is by including, rather than denying, the earlier vision and placing it in sequence that the trilogy creates the conditions for rewriting pastoralism along the lines of a biocentric land ethic. The idea of the garden is definitely given up. The disdain for agrarian pastoralism informs the description of Mexican farmhands who "tended the fields like soiled inmates wandered from some ultimate Bedlam to stand at last hacking in slow and mindless rage at the earth itself" (*Crossing* 235).

What is retained from traditional pastoralism is, for one thing, the utopian quest for a simpler way of life in a nature suitable for subsistence agriculture (such as ranching), and perhaps the insistent codification of nature, ruin, and corpse as allegories of loss. Here as elsewhere in pastoral writing, the congruence between the narrator's and the protagonist's perspectives continues to function in "a complicated interaction between events, the implications of the familiar symbolic landscape, and the protagonist's shifting, all but irremediably ambivalent state of mind. The work of mediation enacted in the 'plot' is even more strenuously undertaken within the protagonist's mind" (Marx, "Pastoralism" 56). Morrison is right when writing that "landscape remains, in *All the Pretty Horses,* a central character and a characterizing agent" (178). Both John Grady and the land function as allegorical figures in the elaboration of the pastoral theme, be it innovative or traditional.

As argued earlier, landscape and characters in McCarthy's pastoralism share fate and status as existential equals. Existential parity, not the promise of transcendence, is the allegorical meaning nature retains is McCarthy's pastoralism. While the romanticist view of wilderness as the sublime habitat of spiritual truth is qualified by the aesthetic parameters of biocentric writing, the romanticist turn toward material nature is intensified into a literally materialist worldview that excludes all dramatic tension between human characters and natural setting. This is the fundamental cause of pastoral failure and melancholia in the trilogy: To subsume human affairs and their history under nature's affairs and natural history in an ecopastoral sense is to render them irrelevant in the great scheme of things.

The biocentrism of this cosmology is elucidated in a scene in which John Grady includes nature in a meditation on the world's dehumanized indifference to human categories of meaning, such as age, race, class, gender, and life itself. At Abuela's grave "he held out his hands as if to steady himself or as if to bless the ground there or perhaps as if to slow the world that was rushing away and seemed to care nothing for the old or the young or rich or poor or dark or pale or he or she. Nothing for their struggles, nothing for their names. Nothing for the living or the dead" (*Horses* 301). As he captures the irrelevance of human concerns to the natural order of things, the narrator (speaking from John Grady's point of view) here erases traditional models of pastoral harmony based on the idea of human stewardship. John Grady repeats this sentiment in *Cities of the Plain* when answering Billy's observation that "[t]he world dont know nothin about your judgment" with "It's worse than that even. It dont care" (219). Simultaneously the world assumes the sentience of any animate life form. This notion of cosmic sentience, symptomatic for the animism of McCarthy's works, is explicitly pronounced by the blind revolutionary veteran in *The Crossing* who "said that the world was sentient to its core and secret and black beyond men's imagining and that its nature did not reside in what could be seen or not seen" (283).[14] The melancholy gaze that is allegorized in the blind man's words, and whose sole structuring principle is the reiteration of loss, thereby reintroduces an egalitarian model of pastoral harmony. In its pessimistic implications, this view is familiar from *Blood Meridian*. It grounds itself in the recognition that all things human and nonhuman are implicated in the universal experience of death and loss, "[t]hat perhaps in his egalitarian way death weighed the gifts of men by their own lights and that in death's eyes the offerings of the poor were the equal of any" (*Cities* 268).

Having said all this, the ecopastoral aspects still need to be pinpointed, for the trilogy does develop a progressive ecopastoral ideology even as dramatizes its failure. Pastoralism then as now defines itself primarily as a literary mode, and the trilogy retains the distinctive elements of the pastoral mode. Thus it bridges the tension between retrospective pastoral nostalgia and its ecopastoral vision. Nonetheless, the term "pastoral" calls for a redefinition in the ecocritical context: "'Pastoral' is used in an extended sense, familiar to Americanists, to refer not to the specific set of obsolescent conventions of the eclogue tradition, but to all literature—poetry or prose, fiction or nonfiction—that celebrates the ethos of nature/rurality over against the ethos of the town or city. This domain includes for present purposes all degrees of rusticity from farm to wilderness" (Buell 23). The states of nature mentioned by Buell as relevant to pastoral literature continue to be based in the "relatively constant features of pastoralism" that Marx lists as "the intricate interplay between the tripartite topography (urban, middle, wild); the narrative or conceptual structure, and the sequence of the protagonist's or speaker's states of mind and feeling" ("Pastoralism" 54). The tripartite topography, however, is redefined to qualify any settlement as civilization and to designate wilderness as anything from virgin forest, to upcountry parkland, to arid desert.

In *All the Pretty Horses,* John Grady's transitions between different states of nature are easy to trace, as are his preferences. During his visit to San Antonio to watch his mother's theater performance he manages to dispel his anxiety that he may have underrated the essence and protocol of urban culture. Having naively expected an alternative existential paradigm rather than mere amusement, his wariness of city life is heightened when he finds new meaning neither in the theater as a cultural institution nor in the representation of that culture by the play's microcosm: "He'd the notion that there would be something in the story itself to tell him about the way the world was or was becoming but there was not. There was nothing in it at all" (21). John Grady's insensitivity to the arts must not be misunderstood as the naiveness of a country boy but read as the picaro's disdain for, and alienation from, codified structures of meaning, such as the aesthetic refinement and etiquette of playhouses. Resembling a parable in its reductive representation of urban civilization, his trip to San Antonio serves merely to confirm his preconceived notions about the realm of the city. So it is without surprise or regret that he heads straight back to the ancestral ranch. Facing the ranch's imminent sale, he and his friend Rawlins literally cross the border into a terra incognita, as suggested by the map they use, which shows "roads and rivers and towns on the American side of the map as far south as the Rio Grande and beyond that all was white" (34). The place they come to after some hardship is a pastoral paradise of the traditional cut, an almost mythical idyll:

> The Hacienda de Nuestra Señora de la Purísima Conceptión was a ranch of eleven thousand hectares situated along the edge of the Bolsón de Cuatro Ciénegas in the state of Coahuila. The western sections ran into the Sierra de Anteojo to elevations of nine thousand feet but south and east the ranch occupied part of the broad barrial or basin floor of the bolsón and was well watered with natural springs and clear streams and dotted with marshes and shallow lakes or lagunas. In the lakes and in the streams were species of fish not known elsewhere on earth and birds and lizards and other forms of life as well all long relict here for the desert stretched away on every side. (97)

The quote also contains two types of wilderness, mountains and desert, and these landscapes represent the prevailing forms of wilderness throughout the trilogy.

Narrative elements indicating pastoral structure include the tripartite plot progression identified by Marx: The protagonist progresses through the three consecutive stages—disengagement, quest, and reintegration. Among the three kinds of recurrent episodes that typify both the pastoral plot and the pastoral protagonist is the "moment when the protagonist enjoys a sense of ecstatic fulfillment, a feeling of calm selfhood and integration with his or her surroundings sometimes including a lover or companion" (Marx, "Pastoralism" 56). Down to the details of lover (Alejandra) and companion (Rawlins), the episodic type matches John Grady's situation at the hacienda before he falls into disgrace and is arrested. The fulfillment in his new profession of breaking and breeding wild mustangs is verbalized in the monologues he addresses to the stallion "in spanish in phrases almost biblical repeating again and again the strictures of a yet untabled law. Soy comandante de las yeguas, he would say, yo y yo sólo" (*Horses* 128).[15] This state of pastoral bliss is unparalleled in *The Crossing* and *Cities of the Plain,* and unsurprisingly Mexico retains its air of a pastoral dream world for John Grady only. Even years later, when working as a ranch hand on McGovern's ranch, he imagines an eventual return to Mexico. His idea that "if there's anything left of this life it's down there" prompts Billy to observe, "I damn sure dont know what Mexico is. I think it's in your head" (*Cities* 218). Billy's experiment with pastoral escape fails to produce anything as idyllic as John Grady's life at the hacienda but marks the beginning of a nomadic lifestyle that continues through the end of the trilogy. It is in the abject wandering of the nomad that Billy finds pastoral sustenance.

The moment consummating the pastoral dream traditionally precipitates a contrary, anticlimactic experience of the pastoral hero that was already discussed in the context of *The Orchard Keeper* and *Child of God*. This second type of pastoral episode (according to Marx) is designed to impel the hero to reconsider his place in nature and to return to civilization either enlightened or disillusioned. The entire third part of *All the Pretty Horses* represents this stage of the pastoral template. John Grady's dream of a bucolic life at the hacienda—working with horses with his best friend, finding the friendship of the simple rustic ranch hands, riding a full-blooded stallion through a sublime wilderness landscape, romancing the hacendado's daughter—suffers a first disillusionment when he is arrested; is shattered during his imprisonment; and finds its seemingly final destruction in the death of the goon he kills in self-defense in prison. Rather than reintegrating himself into society and returning with Rawlins to Texas, however, John Grady crosses into his home country as if trespassing, and he does so only to restore Blevins' horse to its rightful owner. At least in this first installment of the trilogy, John Grady deviates markedly from the conventional course outlined by Marx insofar as he does not back away from "the brutal indifference and immensity of Not-Man" ("Pastoralism" 57). He does not check his pastoral impulse, but commits himself to it for good when retracing his steps back into the Mexican wilderness, "into the darkening land, the world to come" (*Horses* 302). As his meditation at Abuela's grave on the world's indifference exemplifies, he succumbs fully to the moment of truth and takes his cue from its alienating aspect rather than from Rawlins' attempt at resocializing him. But it is for the narrator as much as for John Grady that the Dueña's parable on the idealist's limbo between fact and fiction speaks true: "In the end we all come to be cured of our sentiments. Those whom life does not cure death will. The world is quite ruthless in selecting between the dream and the reality, even where we will not" (*Horses* 238).

That the alienating impulse within the pastoral context emanates less from the wildness of nature than from the ruthlessness of humans becomes even clearer in *The Crossing.* For here it is wilderness incarnate in the wolf that inspires the protagonist's journey, not a quest for a supposedly more pastoral territory. Nowhere does the shift of the ideal pastoral space (from that of the cultivated landscape to that of untouched wilderness) find a more sorrowful and nostalgic articulation than in the emblem of the wolf, an emblem that is picked up again in *Cities of the Plain*. Even though it continues to be idealized as the spirit of the wilderness, its apotheosis in *The Crossing* affects the retrospective vision of stories and old photographs discussed earlier. It is formulated by the narrative voice when Billy buries the slain wolf, with no pretense to be voicing Billy's thoughts or emotions: "He took up her stiff head out of the leaves and held it or he reached to hold what cannot be held, what already ran among the mountains at once terrible and of a great beauty, like flowers that feed on flesh. What blood and bone are made of but can themselves not make on any altar nor by any wound of war. What we may well believe has power to cut and shape and hollow out the dark form of the world surely if wind can, if rain can. But which cannot be held never be held and is no flower but is swift and a huntress and the wind itself is in terror of it and the world cannot lose it" (127). Thus returns, dressed in lyrical diction, the indifferent wilderness spirit that found such prosaic expression in the endemic violence of *Blood Meridian*. It appears to be relinquished by the narrative sense of pastoral as something to be feared and akin to death itself. The old Mexican trapper goes so far as to say "that the wolf is a being of great order and that it knows what men do not: that there is no order in the world save that which death has put there" (*Crossing* 45).

The sentimentality of this passage and others like it exposes the novel to the charge of being invested with a false, hyperbolic pathos. Such an allegation would be hard to defuse even and especially in the face of the emblematic function that the wolf assumes as the aesthetic vessel of the very spirit that is the object of the quests undertaken in each of the trilogy's novels. The very fact that the wolf herself needs protection because the wildness she represents is threatened by the even more ferocious order of human civilization sounds a skeptical note that qualifies the ecopastoral hope in the trilogy even at this early point in the text. The old trapper's comment on the anthropocentrism of men and their ignorance of a metaphysical reality outside its discursive paradigm says as much: "Between their acts and their ceremonies lies the world and in this world the storms blow and the trees twist in the wind and all the animals that God has made go to and fro yet this world men do not see. They see the acts of their own hands or they see that which they name and call out to one another but the world between is invisible to them" (*Crossing* 46). Unsurprisingly, the ending of *Cities of the Plain* returns to the desert setting of *Blood Meridian,* reporting how "[I]n the oncoming years a terrible drought struck west Texas," and how Billy becomes a drifter much like the kid. Here, the pastoral vision of the trilogy regresses until it is reduced to an *ubi sunt* motif that recalls the ruined haciendas in *Blood Meridian:* "Pasture gates stood open and sand drifted in the roads and after a few years it was rare to see stock of any kind and he rode on" (*Cities* 264).

Linked to the assessment of John Grady's and Billy's roles as pastoral protagonist, another type of pastoral episode needs to be rediscussed, namely the machine-in-the-garden motif central to Marx's argument. Marx introduces this episodic type as having no precedent in classic pastoral literature because the pastoral realm is abruptly invaded by "a machine or some other manifest token of the dynamism of modern industrial society" ("Pastoralism" 57). Marx probably overrates the motif's applicability, but it helps to understand the ideological implications of ecopastoralism: "What this episode accomplishes, indeed, is to invert the 'representative event' of the dominant, progressive ideology. So, far from being an occasion for an optimistic vision of history, the sudden intrusion of the machine upon the native landscape evokes feelings of dislocation and anxiety. It reactivates the alienation that had initially provoked the pastoral impulse" ("Pastoralism" 57). To illustrate his point, Marx argues that "[n]o image caught the mood better than the familiar Currier and Ives prints of locomotives hurtling across the western prairie" ("Pastoralism" 37). So it may not be incidental that the opening scene of *All the Pretty Horses* describes John Grady watching a train in an allegory of the industrial invasion of pastoral space (3–4).

Other instances of machines entering pastoral environments in the trilogy include the train that whisks Alejandra away; her father's airplane, which connects the pastoral realm of the hacienda with the metropolitan energy field of Mexico City; the army's takeover of not just Mac's ranch but of the entire valley in *Cities of the Plain;* and the explosion of the atomic bomb at the end of *The Crossing.* The nuclear explosion at Trinity Site is witnessed by Billy from a roadside shack at his moment of deepest dejection, as if this "machine" of gnostic science had indeed become the "evil that can run itself a thousand years" (*Blood Meridian* 19) and had conquered the pastoral dream: "[T]hat noon in which he'd woke was now become an alien dusk and now an alien dark" (*Crossing* 425).

In their reactions to the various machines invading their post-pastoral gardens, John Grady and Billy do not deviate from the parameters of the American pastoral so much as they stretch those parameters to accommodate the logic of a post-humanist universe. Moreover, the melancholy view of history and the allegorical impulse that inform the narrative point of view finally fall into place, for they are the discursive symptoms of the pastoral alienation that Marx associates with the machine's intrusion into the nature idyll. While Marx suggests that the pastoral protagonist tends to yield to the inevitability of progress and restore himself to society when "the new machine technology is made to seem the irreversible motive force of history itself" ("Pastoralism" 57), the trilogy cultivates the machine motif in order to dramatize the pastoral protagonists' continued alienation and melancholia as terminal, as being connected to the abjection of nature itself. Marx delineates another aspect that qualifies the melancholia and alienation of the machine-in-the-garden episode as irremediable and renders the escapist intention of pastoralism itself obsolete: "In the symbolic topography that had previously lent expression to that ancient world view, the locus of power, wealth, hierarchy, sophistication—of the complex world—had been fixed in space . . . : the realm of urbane social life here, the countryside (and wilderness) there. But the new machine power figured forth a fundamental transformation in relations between society and nature. . . . Potential invaders of all sectors of the environment, the forces represented by the new technology necessarily blur (if they do not erase) the immemorial boundary lines between city, countryside, and wilderness" (Marx, "Pastoralism" 58).

The machine's symbolic transgression and obliteration of boundaries in contemporary American pastoralism suggests why John Grady may find no solace in Rawlins' observation that rural Texas "is still good country." John Grady feels compelled to admit "it aint my country," explaining vaguely, "I dont know what happens to country" (*Horses* 299). In the larger context of the trilogy, *Cities of the Plain* shows that the machine has come to stay in the garden in a coexistence of urbanized with pastoral space (the army owns the land, cowboys are driving trucks), and so Jarrett could not have been more right when writing, before the publication of *Cities of the Plain*, "As a series title, The Border Trilogy supersedes the titles of the individual narratives, implying a larger historical continuity or other essential link that presumably connects *All the Pretty Horses* to *The Crossing* as phases of a single, larger narrative" (97). As it patently arranges its plots as first, a quest for a pastoral life (in *All the Pretty Horses*); second, journeys through a pastoral world (in *The Crossing*); and third, the foreclosure of the pastoral vision everywhere (in *Cities of the Plain*), the trilogy tacitly acknowledges the obsolescence of utopian pastoralism. At the same time, its narrative voice retains a residual loyalty to the comic way of wilderness survivalism and to its nomadic representatives.

To understand the shift in pastoral thinking at the bottom of the trilogy's pastoralism—that is, the paradigmatic shift from the idealization of horse ranching in a cultivated landscape, to the idealization of horsemanship in a wild landscape, to the cultural defiance of the wilderness nomad—one has to consider the concept of the protagonists' and narrator's state of mind. In the cases of John Grady and Billy, their negative pastoral experiences may have prompted the protagonists' return to a way of life marked by societal sanction in *Cities of the Plain*. Yet this return is not conciliatory because it has been brought about not by the wilderness episode of conventional pastoralism but by the realization that the influence of civilization (as symbolized in the machine motif) is ubiquitous and that their quests are literally utopian: not from this world. Far from being reconciled to the societal environment they left in search of wilderness, their sense of alienation is exacerbated by the reintegration. If anything, their respective experiences of existential solitude strengthen the bonds of friendship between them.

As discussed in the context of the Southern novels, the pastoral hero has always been defined as a mediator, "a 'liminal figure' who moves back and forth across the borderland between civilization and nature" (Marx, "Pastoralism" 43) and whose "liminal position accounts for his superior grasp of metaphysical reality" ("Pastoralism" 44). This dictum clearly applies to the protagonists of the trilogy who travel back and forth between the closed frontier of Texas and the wilder world of northern Mexico in an essentially nomadic way: homeless migratory horsemen. Marx describes the pastoral hero as being "an ascetic; he is independent, self-sufficient, and, like Henry Thoreau or the rugged western hero of American mythology, a man singularly endowed with the qualities [. . .] that result from his having lived as both a part of, and apart from, nature; from his having lived as both a part of, and apart from, society" ("Pastoralism" 43). But while John Grady and Billy partake of this dual implication of the pastoral figure in both the wildness of nature and the culture of civilization, they are at home in neither world. Unlike Ownby in *The Orchard Keeper,* whose mystic immersion into wilderness makes him nature's familiar, they fail to find fulfillment in the wilderness. They also fail to mediate between wilderness and horse ranch pastoralism, to say nothing of urban civilization. Nonetheless, both are constructed as ecopastoral heroes. The hardships they suffer induce the spiritual condition for the gradual acquisition of an ecopastoral sense of self. The genesis of the ecocentric self becomes the true object of their quests, not an alternative way of life in nature. Hence the trilogy seems preoccupied less with an aesthetic of optical democracy but with one of spiritual democracy throughout the animate world: Through the metaphysical consolidation of his animism, the narrator moves one step away from a materialist biocentrism and one step closer to a nature mysticism that reconnects to McCarthy's first novel.

The evolution of this ecopastoral sense of self is gradual. Initially, each of the two pastoral heroes sets out on his respective quest not so much out of necessity but out of his own volition and a picaresque craving for adventure. Unlike the simple country people of Mexico whom they encounter and depend on for sympathy, John Grady and Billy nowhere become unselfconscious enough to forget their own cultural background. They never cease to reflect on the distance they have put between it and themselves. Like the protagonists of other American pastorals, they are marked by a "double consciousness" that "presents a vision of a disengaged, unworldly life, to be sure, but one that is entertained by a sophisticate" (Marx, "Pastoralism" 56). Although it might be going too far to call John Grady or Billy "sophisticates," their escapist journeys and quests originate in a conscious thought process that is motivated first by their enthusiasm for a life in the saddle, then by their increasing disillusionment. It is precisely their disillusionment and alienation that motivates their intellectual and emotional development into the alternative pastoral type of the ecopastoral hero, or *eco-hero*.

Placing him within the tripartite narrative structure of the heroic journey (which parallels Marx's tripartite structure of the pastoral plot), Tim Poland derives the term eco-hero from the traditional figure of the mythical hero. The heroic self is achieved as the hero's boon for his community, rather than for himself, in the course of quest, trial, and atonement. Poland defines the eco-hero's sense of self as "a synthesis of . . . [the] image of the heroic Self with the image of the relational Self emergent in deep ecology, or *ecosophy* as it is referred to here."[16] Poland summarizes the term ecosophy as follows:

> Suffice it to say that, unlike mainstream ecological perspectives focusing on the preservation of resources and natural beauty for the use and pleasure of the human community, ecosophy is an ontological perspective that rejects the traditional Western view of "man-in-environment." It favors a world view that situates humanity "in integrity," that perceives humanity as part of, not separate from, all living forms, that sees humanity in relation to the ecosphere, not upon it. In addition to the central concept of existence as relational rather than individual, ecosophy recognizes all components of the ecosphere as having intrinsic value for their own sake. This stance, accordingly, seeks and nurtures diversity and

> complexity and fights against all forms of pollution, class hierarchy, and outside threats to bioregional autonomy. (Poland 196)

Essentially, the eco-hero translates into that pastoral figure of recent Western American writing who has come to adopt an "eco-centric Self" (Poland 197) in place of the egocentric self. He defines himself in his dealings with nature by way of a relational quality that aligns the human self in an egalitarian way with its environment, rather than imposing the former upon the latter. Morrison's notion of landscape as character in *All the Pretty Horses* (178) does not begin to unfold its full meaning until brought into context with this, the ecopastoral worldview that for the trilogy evolves out of the aesthetic of "optical democracy" discussed in the chapter on *Blood Meridian*. Attending this changed perception of nature—that emerges in *The Orchard Keeper*—is the shift of the pastoral self-image "from 'man the conqueror' of the ecosphere to 'man the biotic citizen' of it" (Poland 196),[17] that is, a biocentric alignment of the picaro's comic way of personal survival with the idea of an ecologically inclusive survivalism.

The figure of the eco-hero has evolved not in American pastoralism in general but in *Western* American pastoralism, in texts that stylize wilderness into nature's last stronghold against man. Taking its survivalist cues from the Native American way of life, the Western hero (including the gunslinger) has always tried to adapt to, and survive in, terrain hostile to man, to live off the land, to cover his tracks, to leave places as undisturbed as possible. The Western eco-hero differs from the traditional hero of the Western only insofar as he effects this existential acclimatization not out of an individual but out of a collective survival instinct. The emergence of the Western eco-hero adds an ecological dimension to the concept of the traditional Western hero.[18] It is John Grady's and Billy's integrity and interactive sense of self that sets them apart from Lester and the kid.

As sensitive interaction with the land constitutes the condition for survival in the desert, it is not despite the bleakness of the desert landscape of the Southwest, but because of it, that Western American pastoralism dispenses with the anthropocentric idea of man's colonizing of wilderness into a garden. The regional reinterpretation of the meaning of pastoralism evidently turns on a changed attitude toward the concept of wilderness. The term "wilderness" here associates environments that defy human habitation (as epitomized in the desert landscape): "Wilderness is land showing minimal human influence" (Love 202).[19] In conjunction with the progressive destruction of nature for the exploitation of resources—that is, the very process that has brought about the ongoing revival of the pastoral mode in Western American writing—the pastoral domain appears to have moved from the central position of wilderness-turned-garden and "rural landscape as the locus of stability and value" (Love 203) to wilderness itself. This development cannot come as a surprise, for American pastoralism contained from the start a "gap between scrabbling actuality and picturesque Jeffersonian ideal, according to which the ethos of farming empowers, not frustrates, the pursuit of culture." Starting with Thoreau, "pastoral hedonism becomes an indictment of the deadening pragmatism of agrarian economy" (Buell 12), and even *The Orchard Keeper* and *Outer Dark* suggest as much. The ideological shift in pastoralism was imminent but not realized until ecology had been firmly established in the natural sciences. Germinating the old seed of pastoral self-doubt, recent ecological concern and the fear of an impending environmental disaster have "radicalized the pastoral experience" (Love 203) through a fundamental reconsideration of wilderness as a space of precarious equilibrium rather than a barren wasteland. "If the key terms for relatively untrammeled nature in the past were *simplicity* and *permanence,* those terms have shifted in an ecologically-concerned present to *complexity* and *change*. Instead of seeing wilderness as an appealing but ultimately impossible alternative, it is now increasingly studied and interpreted as the model of a complex diversity and a new pattern for survival" (Love 202–203). The ideology behind this radicalism suggests that pastoralism today needs to be understood as not merely a mediating way of life in harmony with both the natural and the societal environment, but as a state of metaphysical awareness as well. The pastoral ethos has undergone an analogous shift from an anthropocentric view of nature as a material stockpile to a post-humanist, materialist view of man and nature as being equal and codependent. "Distance was the hallmark of the old pastoral artist" (Love 203), whereas the ecopastoralist writes not from outside but from within the natural world.

The trilogy reduces the man-nature hierarchy gradually to a zero level of shared materiality (rather than to a level of shared wildness as in *Child of God* or *Blood Meridian*). In *All the Pretty Horses,* the impending demise of the old pastoral vision is figuratively captured in the aspect of John Grady's moribund father (who no longer even lives on the Grady ranch) when he and John Grady ride together one last time: "Looking over the country with those sunken eyes as if the world out there had been altered or made suspect by what he'd seen of it elsewhere. As if he might never see it right again. Or worse did see it right at last. See it as it had always been, would forever be" (23). Situating John Grady within our ecopastoral reading, the new egalitarian view of the world "as it had always been, would forever be" is allegorized in the novel's man-horse theme, invoking a metaphysical unity between John Grady and horses. The assumption that the man-horse relationship represents its central theme is borne out by John Grady's centaur-like "half-man, half-horse" (Morrison 181) quality, the closing image of John Grady and his horse as "their long shadow passed in tandem like the shadows of a single being" (302). It is also confirmed by the image of John Grady—contrasting with that of his father (quoted above)[20]—"who rode on slightly before him sat a horse not only as if he'd been born to it which he was but as if were he begot by malice or mischance into some queer land where horses never were he would have found them anyway" (*Horses* 23).

Resembling a pastoral apotheosis, the image functions as a mere prelude to a number of instances of John Grady's communicating with horses in rather unconventional ways. The progressive intensification of the John-horse relationship illustrates (on the plot level) the thematic development (on the secondary level). His patronizing, if fair, behavior in the early horse-breaking scenes is still characterized by the master-subject relationship of traditional animal husbandry. When it is said in *All the Pretty Horses* that "he did not stop speaking to the horse at all, speaking in a low steady voice and telling it all that he intended to do" (103–104), that he "talked to it just as if it were neither crazy nor lethal" (106), that "[h]e thought the horse had handled itself well and as he rode he told it so" (125), or that he talks to the purebred stallion "softly in spanish" (126), these monologues go hardly beyond the baby talk commonly addressed to domestic animals. John Grady's reverence for horses in the pastoral—not *ecopastoral*—realm of the hacienda is still of a degree shared by the Mexican hands and foreman ("like John Grady he would talk to the horse and often make promises to him and he never lied to the horse," 127). While this reverence prepares for the shift in pastoral worldview, it is not until later in the novel that John Grady's revelations regarding horses acquire a fantastic touch and begin to read like allegorical monologues on a relational, ecopastoral ethos.

The moment patently launching John Grady's transition from pastoral to ecopastoral worldview in *All the Pretty Horses* seems to occur during a campfire conversation of the young horsemen with the old-timer Luis. The latter, a veteran cavalryman, assumes the role of John Grady's mentor in introducing him to the mystical notion that "the souls of horses mirror the souls of men more closely than men suppose" (111). Poland points out that the allegorical hero is traditionally guided during his quest by an advisory figure (like Dante being guided by Virgil and Beatrice), and that "the guide's obligation is to show the hero the way to the inclusive vision and the acquisition of the boon, not to bestow it upon him" (203). Analogously, John Grady's ecopastoral vision, evolving later in the novel, seems to come as the result of a mental process triggered by Luis's words. Even his dream of a heaven of horses (161) seems to recall Rawlins' question about whether " there was a heaven for horses," in answer to which Luis "shook his head and said that a horse had no need of heaven" (111). In an ecosophical reformulation of Donne's words, "any man's *death* diminishes *me*, because I am involved in *Mankind*" (441), Luis elevates the horse to an emblematic manifestation of the oversoul: "Lastly he said that he had seen the souls of horses and that it was a terrible thing to see. He said that it could be seen under certain circumstances attending the death of a horse because the horse shares a common soul and its separate life only forms it out of all horses and makes it mortal. He said that if a person understood the soul of the horse then he would understand all horses that ever were" (111). Even at this point John Grady appears to be aware of environmental destruction and lost continuity, because he asks Luis in his own parabolic manner "if it were not true that should all horses vanish from the face of the earth the soul of the horse would not also perish for there would be nothing out of which to replenish it" (111). The very real concern underlying this question, and the fact that

Luis passes it off as a moot issue tantamount to blasphemy, suggests an incipient fissure between the old man's romantic pastoralism and John Grady's nascent ecopastoral awareness.

His potential affinity for a wilderness pastoralism surfaces early on when "[h]e lay a long time listening to the others breathing in their sleep while he contemplated the wildness about him, the wildness within" (60). But the relational quality of the ecohero does not fully manifest itself in John Grady's thinking until after the structural anticlimax, which is constituted jointly by the incidents in prison, the conference with the Dueña, and the loss of Alejandra. The final chapter of *All the Pretty Horses* contains the following example: "Blevins' horse was breathing with slow regularity and his stomach was warm and his shirt damp from the horse's breath. He found he was breathing in rhythm with the horse as if some part of the horse were within him breathing and then he descended into some deeper collusion for which he had not even a name" (266). The observation that John Grady cannot name this deeper harmony recalls the ineffable continuity discussed in the context of melancholia: a continuity that precedes human existence and that represents a loss that can be neither remembered nor forgotten. This continuity enters into the allegory on John Grady's meditation of the horse, and it radically differs from the man-controlled, culturally codified collaboration between domestic animal and man that marks Luis's ideal of good horsemanship. Rather, the continuity thus allegorized invokes the lost harmony between man and nature. Another dream image may substantiate this reading of the horse as a still wild creature heraldic of the ecopastoral vision. John Grady's transition from the semi-sleep into the dream state is fleeting, unacknowledged by punctuation or temporal separation:

> In his sleep he could hear the horses stepping among the rocks and he could hear them drink from the shallow pools in the dark where the rocks lay smooth and rectilinear as the stones of ancient ruins and the water from their muzzles dripped and rang like water dripping in a well and in his sleep he dreamt of horses and the horses in his dream moved gravely among the tilted stones like horses come upon an antique site where some ordering of the world had failed and if anything had been written

> on the stones the weathers had taken it away again and the horses were wary and moved with great circumspection carrying in their blood as they did the recollection of this and other places where horses once had been and would be again. (*Horses* 280)

Nicely capturing allegory's timeless rewriting of anterior texts, this dream image shows how the human master plan inscribed on the stones of the natural, pastoral world has been eroded over time, whereas the horse as an equine emblem of nature's self-renewing continuity remains impervious to erosion. Being an animal half domesticated and half wild, the horse incarnates the mediating worldview of ecopastoralism.

Ultimately, the horse-man theme implies that the two contrasting profiles of father and son early on in *All the Pretty Horses* anticipate this generational shift from traditional to ecosophical pastoralism. The passage cited is immediately succeeded by the *ubi sunt* allegory of an abandoned domain of the old agrarian order, "the ruins of an old ranch on that stony mesa" (23). The context of this motif reiterates the earlier conclusion that melancholy and allegorical elements in the trilogy are superimposed on the text proper in the form of a meta-narrative, and that this meta-narrative manifests itself most clearly in certain pastoral emblems usurping the protagonists' point of view while originating with the narrative voice. These emblematic allegories can be said to form an arc comprising images of both pastoral harmony and pastoral loss. For example, when John Grady and Rawlins set out on their pastoral quest in *All the Pretty Horses*, an allegory stylizes the episode into a liturgical ascension to a prelapsarian paradise of mystical quality:

> They rode out on the high prairie where they slowed the horses to a walk and the stars swarmed around them out of the blackness. They heard somewhere in that tenantless night a bell that tolled and ceased where no bell was and they rode out on the round dais of the earth which alone was dark and no light to it and which carried their figures and bore them up into the swarming stars so that they rode not under but among them and they rode at once jaunty and circumspect, like thieves newly loosed in that dark electric, like young thieves in a

> glowing orchard, loosely jacketed against the cold and
> ten thousand worlds for the choosing. (30)

Eventually, however, the land they traverse (allegorized here as a garden, the pastoral ideal) appears as the garden fallen along with mankind, fallen not because of man's religious failings but strictly because of his secular ones. In the metaphysics of ecopastoralism—which implicates not nature in man's fate, but nature and man in the same, shared fate—original sin returns as man's hubris of exploiting the earth for his own ends. Within a non-anthropocentric universe, evil emanates not from a serpent tempting man to become like God, but from man taking advantage of God's instruction to "replenish the earth, and subdue it" (Gen. 1:28). Predictably, *All the Pretty Horses* reflects the obsolescence of traditional pastoralism in images of the New Adam and his ruined garden:

> He rode through a grove of apple trees gone wild and brambly and he picked an apple as he rode and bit into it and it was hard and green and bitter. . . . He rode past the ruins of an old cabin. . . . There was a strange air to the place. As of some site where life had not succeeded. (225–26)

What makes this image allegorical is the typological reference to anterior texts involving gardens lost and mourned. While referring to something explicitly absent—here, the former beauty of the garden—the allegory implies the presence of the pastoral dream as a notion always already subjected to erasure by the melancholy gaze. Unlike comparable *ubi sunt* motifs in pastoral literature, the garden is shown here in its moment of erasure as a utopian vision no longer even desirable: The passage refers to classic pastoralism itself as to some discursive site "where life had not succeeded."

The ecopastoral alternative is suggested in surrealistic dream images such as the passage on the heaven of horses. This and the previous textual example both constitute allegories. The first is informed by an apocalyptic cosmology, that is, a *vanitas* vision of a lost pastoral past; the second by a redemptive vision of a celestial world ordered to suit an equally utopian ecopastoral ideal. The dream image makes for a parable of an ecopastoral, rather than just pastoral, utopia because John Grady runs among the horses as their equal not their master "and there was nothing else at all in that high world and they moved all of them in a resonance . . . which is the world itself and which cannot be spoken but only praised" (*Horses* 161–62). This powerful allegory—consisting of a single sentence half a page in length—connects directly to the apotheosis of the wolf's spirit (*Crossing* 127) quoted earlier. Both the allegorical character of the vision and its underlying melancholia testify to the fact that its object, pastoral harmony between man and nature, "cannot be spoken." It is discursively unattainable because the symbolic order of discourse is, per se, logocentric.

Here as elsewhere in the trilogy the narrator's melancholy gaze stylizes nature into an icon of loss. Similarly, baroque literature treats nature as an allegory in itself, implicated in the human fall from grace and therefore inherently sorrowful and silent. In the context of allegoresis, pastoralism works two ways: At the same time that the retreat out of a corrupt civilization into pastoral nature is motivated by the sorrow felt over a world gone to ruin, nature itself induces melancholia firstly because the pastoral ideal of the nature idyll defies reification, and secondly because the pastoral dream itself is always already subject to the pastoral break (the intrusion of death, evil, or technology). In the trilogy, the grief in nature is caused by the inherent futility of all pastoral quests, including ecopastoral ones.

Among the emblems of pastoral loss that recur quasi-independently of the protagonists' sorrow is John Grady's vision of the Comanche—representatives of an ecopastoral way of life—"like a dream of the past" (*Horses* 5). As he admits to Magdalena, this vision used to haunt him during his boyhood, when "the ghosts of the Comanches would pass all about him on their way to the other world again and again" (*Cities* 205). Another such instance is the twilight scene concluding *All the Pretty Horses*. It strikes a note of pastoral nostalgia by stylizing a bull (the strongest of domesticated beasts, but out of place in the desert) into an allegory on the demise of traditional pastoralism: "In the evening a wind came up and reddened all the sky before him. There were few cattle in that country because it was barren country indeed yet he came at evening upon a solitary bull rolling in the dust against the bloodred sunset like an animal in sacrificial torment. The bloodred dust blew down out of the sun" (302)[21]. In a more sorrowful way (because the destruction of wilderness, the last sanctuary in the ecopastoral context, causes an even deeper sense of loss), the motif is picked up again in *Cities of the Plain* when old Mr. Johnson recalls the last time that he heard a wolf, and the metaphysical implication of the motif is made explicit: "But I guess I was always what you might call superstitious. I know I damn sure wasnt religious. And it had always seemed to me that somethin can live and die but that the kind of thing they were was always there. I didnt know you could poison that: I aint heard a wolf howl in thirty odd years. I dont know where you'd have to go to hear one. There may not be any such a place" (126).

In *Cities of the Plain,* even the dream that the relatively pristine wildness of Mexico might yet offer a pastoral retreat is abandoned when Billy dismisses it as John Grady's personal pipedream. Moreover, even the ecopastoral vision is subjected to erasure and melancholia, not only because its avatar, John Grady, loses his life, but because other allegorical representatives of ecopastoralism are shown not as avatars but as epigonic relicts of the past: The Native Americans whom John Grady envisions in imaginary encounters blend into the set like an allegorical supporting cast who "stood and watched him pass and watched him vanish upon that landscape solely because he was passing. Solely because he would vanish" (*Horses* 301). The question of whether Native Americans still camped out in West Texas as late as the 1950s is made irrelevant by the fact that these figures are nothing but a mirage, a self-referential allegory on a defunct ecopastoral way of life. Because John Grady remains unsure of how to realize his potential pastoral awareness, these twilight reveries identify his ecopastoral status as equally allegorical, anachronistic, and, moreover, susceptible to an obsolete romanticism.

The environmental critique contained in the Border Trilogy hardly goes beyond a negative assessment of each and every form of pastoralism "as of some site where life had not succeeded." The trilogy's ecological statement amounts to little more than a metaphysical flirt with wilderness. Except for John Grady's dream of living alone with Magdalena in a cabin on the range, *Cities of the Plain* is actually free of any affirmative ecopastoralism whatsoever. Indeed, McCarthy's ecopastoral allegoresis may well exhaust itself in reinstating nature as a literal fact and liberating it from its reduction to an object of human appropriation and appreciation.[22] If this were true, the uncompromising egalitarianism of death in

Blood Meridian would ring even truer, from a biocentric point of view. While ecopastoral writing in general seems "to have provided a growing contemporary audience with that sense of an ecological reality check they do not find elsewhere" (Love 204), the trilogy does little more than ground man and nature equally in the absolutely indifferent and absolutely shared materiality of existence. But the lack of ecosophical commitment neither supports nor contradicts any ecocritical argument, for the pastoral genre is culturally constructed as an imaginary escapism, not as an ideology. Even ecopastoralism cannot be discussed except as a literary construct, and it would be "a mistake to think of pastoralism as chiefly concerned with the defense of physical nature itself" (Marx, "Pastoralism" 66).

This way, the compositional unity of the Border Trilogy manifests itself. Pastoral subject, melancholy mood, and allegoresis interact to redefine American pastoralism along ecosophical lines while subjecting it to the typological nostalgia that characterizes all antecedent forms of pastoralism. Structurally, the trilogy approximates the quality of a palimpsest since allegoresis serves as the basic aesthetic principle. Read in this context, McCarthy's offhand remark that "books are made out of books" refers the reader to the novels' rhythmic erasing and rewriting of antecedent meanings and pre-texts.

Subsuming contemporary ecopastoralism under the melancholia of traditional pastoralism and choosing an allegorical form for this undertaking represents the truly unique aspect of the trilogy. Rather than making any activist commitment, the Trilogy reconnects to the animism of *The Orchard Keeper*. What McCarthy salvages from both the ruins of pastoralism and the leveling effect that ecopastoralism has on his literary landscape are the narratives themselves, the smaller tales they contain, and the act of storytelling as such, both as dramatized *in* the novels and as practiced *by* the novels. Thus the trilogy mediates between the positive force of pastoral identification with the land and the negative force of pastoral melancholia by advancing two solutions, one answering to the alienation of being a discontinuous part of a cosmic continuity; the other answering to the alienation of the pastoral subject. The first is the extension of picaresque nomadism beyond the novel's ending in relational identification of the human protagonist with nature: the strictly secular teleology of ecopastoralism.

The second solution is that of the storyteller, who literally comes to terms with his melancholia by allegorizing it, and who thus attains omnipotent control over his internal world of sorrow. More than in *All the Pretty Horses,* these alternatives, the nomad's drifting and the storyteller's work of memory, figure in *The Crossing,* what with Billy Parham's triple journey and the number of interpolated tales. And while John Grady succumbs to his pastoral fantasies in *Cities of the Plain,* Billy remains a nomad and a storyteller. Perhaps this is how the dedication concluding the Trilogy is to be read: "The story's told / Turn the page" (*Cities* 293). If we turn to other pastoral stories, we are bound to hear identical tales of sorrow and solace.

Conclusion

Animism over Ecosophy

> I conceive of no flourishing and heroic elements of Democracy in the United States, or of Democracy maintaining itself at all, without the Nature-element forming a main part—to be its health-element and beauty-element—to really underlie the whole politics, sanity, religion and art of the New World.
>
> Walt Whitman, *Specimen Days*

Interpretations of literature must concede that ultimately they are mere reiterations of that literature, and reductive ones at that. There is no way to retell the novels of Cormac McCarthy in a way that would make them more accessible, less multifaceted. Like all great works of fiction they are polyglot mosaics that lend themselves to discussions of specific themes and aspects but resist comprehensive surveys. The foregoing review of McCarthy's pastoralism addresses the theme of melancholia and the allegorical composition throughout, but it neglects, among other things, McCarthy's use of idiom and historical detail, or his sense of place. The resultant chronicle of McCarthy's evolving ecopastoralism suggests, however, that the relational quality of this pastoralism integrates social, historical, and psychological aspects into a holistic chronotope of wilderness.[1] In closing, these insights allow for an assessment of the author's place in American pastoralism.

Any definition of American pastoralism necessarily interrelates with the aesthetic representation of the idea of America as "nature's nation." From the Puritan reflections on the settlement of North America as an exodus into wild country, to Jeffersonian agrarianism, to Turner's frontier thesis, to conservationism, to the environmental movement of the late twentieth century, Americans have always sought to define their nationhood via their relationship to the land, no matter whether the country's essence be identified as garden or wilderness, as amber waves of grain or purple mountains' majesty. The pastoral promise associated with the uncivilized New World conditions the literary representation of American nature, as often as not, through aesthetic strategies of ideologically committed character. Nature in American pastoralism has come to function as a typological chronotope, an allegory. It is hardly incidental that allegorical discourse has played a key role from the very inception of the escapist concept of America as a promised land because it answered to the need to root in historical precedent or material analogy a society that—being as it were a new society—lacked a history of its own. In the representation of America as a discursive construct, allegoresis could do what historiography could not, namely match place with history, a terra incognita with an expedient legacy. From the start the meaning of American democracy tied in closely with the meaning of its landscape in the shared allegory of prosperity, liberty and equality. And from the start American pastoralism has been prescriptive and cosmological.

The principal flaw of allegorical discourse, its notorious bias, becomes its greatest merit when purposefully deployed, if at the expense of realism (in literary representation, not political implementation). If the founding of America as "nature's nation" is stylized as a wedding of virgin (noncultivated) land with the virgin (ideologically innovative) paradigm of American democracy, then any representation of the land and its geophysical parameters reflects on, and thereby represents, the land's inhabitants, bequeathing upon both an imaginary, allegorical kinship. Then wilderness translates into political freedom. The American pastoral is culturally specific insofar as it projects into the landscape an equalizing quality that parallels the egalitarian tenets of the Constitution.

Thoreau's romanticist sense of self is extracted from his nature meditations (as is the idea of civil disobedience). In romanticism, sublime wilderness stands in for the oversoul, and men become equal in nature just as they are equal in the face of God (hence the abolitionist tendencies in transcendentalism and transcendentalist differences from Southern antebellum pastoralism). In American literature, some of the intrinsically democratic and individualist American ideals, such as the allegorical figures of the self-reliant yeoman and the New Adam, originate in the pastoral analogy of egalitarian nature with political equality. The energy and sublime truth of wilderness in romanticist writing, for instance, corresponds directly to the moral integrity of Cooper's Natty Bumppo. The same goes for the relationship between Zane Grey's Lassiter and the moralizing Western landscape. In today's ecopastoralism it is again the egalitarian quality of nature, seen from a post-humanist point of view, that inspires the idea of "optical democracy."

What is indigenous in American pastoralism, then, is that while pastoral writing is generally associable with alienation and escape from civilization, the American pastoral since the age of romanticism (at the latest) has been marked instead by a positive identification of American civic virtue with the raw energy of the American wilderness. The lone backwoodsman, the cowboy, the farmer, even the drifter, seem to represent the American spirit more than the urban citizen. This notion of American man being an intrinsic part of the American landscape has shown itself to be remarkably resilient in weathering ideological shifts: The transcendentalist immersion into wilderness differs from the biocentric land ethic of ecopastoralism only in the latter's posthumanist approach. Ironically, the easy co-optation of the most radically anti-civilizational, and even anti-anthropocentric, pastoral writers—such as Thoreau, John Muir, Aldo Leopold, or Barry Lopez—presents the greatest danger for American ecopastoralism. But it has also presented one of the most potent means of effecting a change in public awareness toward ecological concerns.

In short, the egalitarian tendencies inherent in American pastoralism clearly accommodate the biocentric shift in today's nature writing and prepare for McCarthy's aesthetic of optical democracy. In view of the foregoing discussion, however, McCarthy's novels seem to resist any progressive ecopastoralism based in ecosophy. While foregrounding an egalitarian pastoral cosmology and acknowledging the interrelatedness of all ecological components, their narrative voices seem curiously indifferent to any active endorsement of environmentalist awareness. In fact, the narrative indifference to the failure of its own ecopastoral vision (such as in the Border Trilogy), the regressive ecopastoralism of certain points of view (such as those of Arthur Ownby and Lester Ballard), and the complete absence of dramatized environmentalist activism (such as is suggested in Edward Abbey's *The Monkey Wrench Gang*), appear to simulate the indifference of nature itself that is displayed in the novels. The all-pervasive melancholia of McCarthy's narrators, which deviates from the affirmative or defiant spirit of much ecopastoral literature, dominates the narration to a degree that would threaten to render the ecopastoral turn altogether incongruous if it did not open onto an ulterior angle.

Animism over Ecosophy

It has become established procedure to approach McCarthy's novels from an ecocritical angle, and ecocriticism goes a long way in explaining aspects of genre, theme, and setting. Yet the discussion is not becoming any easier, but more complex, because an ecocritical interpretation calls in turn for specification of any one of a number of ecopastoral worldviews. The ecocritical meaning isolated in McCarthy's work may actually do nothing so much as reflect the ecological shift within the critical community, a shift that originates in the schools of post-structuralism and New Historicism as much as in environmentalism. Yet a book like *The Orchard Keeper,* which is invested with ecopastoral meaning just like the Border Trilogy, has yielded deeply meaningful interpretations of the novel's nature mysticism prior to its recent ecocritical reception, and these early interpretations continue to be meaningful. While the anti-hegemonic tendencies of postmodernism more or less condition the post-humanist underpinnings of recent ecopastoralism, McCarthy's allegorical rhetoric clearly avoids the semantic ambiguity of postmodern literature. Its preference for typological reference creates intertextual palimpsests that are easier to decode than postmodern pastiches because the interpretative culs-de-sac that McCarthy's writings may present form part of an iconographic tradition: the world as stage, death personified, fate, the magic of names, and the trickster, among other emblems. The use of antecedent (originally religious or mythological) iconography is mystifying insofar as it remains metaphysically meaningful within the narrative contexts even as the narratives erase its transcendental meaning. The use of such iconography suggests that the relational quality of McCarthy's ecopastoralism has more in common with the older idea of mystical immersion in nature than with present-day biocentrism. It partakes of the animism of myth and fable, in which man's interaction with animals and landscape harbors a deeper level of meaning beyond logocentric signification, and in this way acquires an epic dimension.

McCarthy is above everything else an allegorist—a storyteller—whose relational sense of self makes him a mystic before making him a nature writer. In effect, his mystic animism refers the democratic aspiration that grounds American pastoralism back to a heritage that has at times been ignored, but which has been rehabilitated in the context of the ecocritical debate: the egalitarian cosmology of Native American myth.

> Native American writing at times shows even greater pastoral radicalism . . . when instead of presenting merely a scene of exclusion from a familiar arcadia, it redefines the terms of that arcadia in the process. The route, for instance, by which the protagonist in Leslie Silko's *Ceremony* (1977) is transformed from broken-down GI to tribal savior is through a retreat to nature that reorients him by putting him in touch with primal power, expressed through a symbolic geography grounded in an intricately culture-specific sense of place accessible to mainstream readers only through scholarly meditations, and resting upon a communalistic land ethic alien to American assumptions about property rights. (Buell 13)

Animism and nature mysticism are not Native American prerogatives, but Native American mythology represents the indigenous domain of such a "symbolic geography" and " communalistic land ethic" in American literature. Far from suggesting that McCarthy's epigonic Indians attach him to Native American literature, this merely says that McCarthy's ecopastoralism betrays more affinity with Native American animism (and European mysticism) than with the ecopastoral regionalism of the American South or West.

Native Americans, wherever they occur in McCarthy's novels, represent agents of an older cultural paradigm: holistic, animistic, and resigned to the transience of individual existence. They are also representative of the anachronistic, always-already-defunct nature of any pastoral dream. As nice as it would be to qualify this observation to exempt recent ecopastoralism, McCarthy's pastoralism claims no exemption from the obsolescence of older pastoral paradigms. A differentiation that Karl Kroeber offers regarding the environmental awareness of ancient cultures seems to apply: "As an admirer of ancient Greek civilization and for some time now a student of Native American cultures, I have been impressed by these 'early' cultures' sensitive understanding of interrelations between human activities and the natural environment—as well as their perceptions into the workings of natural systems. [. . .] But neither ancient Greeks nor Native Americans, nor anyone before the nineteenth century, had, or could have had, a systematically ecological understanding of nature—as the barrenness of the Greek landscape and the abandoned cliff dwellings in the Southwest poignantly testify" (27). McCarthy's ecopastoralism equally neglects to include "a systematically ecological understanding of nature." It bespeaks instead an aesthetic commitment to older versions of the relational pastoral, favoring animism over ecosophy, and cultivating the attendant narrative melancholia. In his narrators, the presence of Native Americans, such as that of the Tarahumara in the quote below, inspires not nostalgia over the desolation in the garden but a distanced contemplation of "the diminutive progress of all things in the valley" (*Child* 170). And in this melancholic equanimity lies the essence of McCarthy's pastoral vision: "The indians were dark almost to blackness and their reticence and their silence bespoke a view of a world provisional, contingent, deeply suspect. They had about them a wary absorption, as if they observed some hazardous truce. They seemed in a state of improvident and hopeless vigilance. Like men committed upon uncertain ice" (*Crossing* 193).

Notes

Introduction

1. Not discussed, then, are McCarthy's two short stories, "A Wake for Susan" (1957) and "A Drowning Incident" (1958); the TV drama *The Gardener's Son* (1977); and the drama *The Stonemason* (1998).

2. Arnold writes that *Suttree* contains more than 150 named characters, many of whom are based on historic personae ("Naming" 57). Incidentally, McAnally is already mentioned in *The Orchard Keeper* as the destination of Sylder's whiskey runs (29). McCarthy's father, a lawyer, served on the legal board of the Tennessee Valley Authority, so the novel's rebellious undertones suggest autobiographical motives. Also, the fact that, like McCarthy, Suttree spent time at the local university explains the protagonist's prolixity.

3. *The Divine Comedy,* Canto XIII. The parallel is pointed out by Arnold ("Naming" 68, n. 21).

4. For the parallels between *Suttree* and works by Camus and Eliot, see Shelton's essay; for the parallels to Dante, see Arnold's essay "Naming, Knowing and Nothingness."

5. The intertextuality is made explicit when Suttree dreams of stopping in front of a watchmaker's shop and watching the timepieces arrest themselves in his presence (453–54). The fact that Quentin drowns himself finds a meaningful analogy in Suttree's fear of drowning and his mortification when a suicide is pulled from the river and he perceives that "the dead man's watch was still running" (10).

6. McCarthy's knowledge of James is mentioned in Garry Wallace's problematic but nonetheless useful article "Meeting McCarthy" (138). This information suggests that McCarthy carefully calculates the narrative effect of his narrators' melancholia, rather than drawing on any personal sense of disenchantment.

7. Suttree's realizations that "there is one Suttree and one Suttree only" (461) and "[a] man is all men" (422) are compared by Bell to "Walt Whitman speaking in a new idiom and time" (*Achievement* 110).

8. The quote reconnects to "The Waste Land" in which Eliot speaks of "[t]hese fragments I have shored against my ruins" (504). The intertextuality confirms that Suttree's quest for meaning and self is informed more by a modernist crisis of meaning than by the postmodernist contestation of all hegemonic structures of meaning.

9. Sullivan's critique of *Suttree* is a case in point: "The shape of the novel is amorphous, even for McCarthy, whose long suit has never been dramatic structure. One gets the impression that McCarthy walks through the world cramming his brain with experience both actual and vicarious and then goes to work and gives everything back, scene upon scene, the devil take the hindmost" ("Citizens" 341).

10. Macbeth's words are these: "Life's but walking shadow; a poor player / That struts and frets his hour upon the stage, / And then is heard no more: it is a tale / Told by an idiot, full of sound and fury, / Signifying nothing" (act 5, scene 5). The lines are so familiar that McCarthy could hardly have created the image without having intended the reader's inference of the intertextuality and the attendant melancholia.

11. The context is Suttree's love affair with Wanda; his feeling of cosmic harmony recalls *Leaves of Grass* in which Whitman writes: "And I know [. . .] that all the men ever born are also my brothers . . . and the women my sisters and lovers, / And that a kelson of the creation is love" (31).

Chapter 1

1. Parallels to Faulkner's fiction are discussed by Ditsky, Jarrett, Prescott, Ragan, Sullivan ("Worlds"), and Trachtenberg, among others.

2. Although the image of the tree of life is probably universal, it does have a specifically American ring as intertextual analogies can be found, for instance, in Neihardt's *Black Elk Speaks* (1932): "There is no center any longer, the sacred tree is dead" (230).

3. The manual is mentioned once more in *The Crossing*, though the title is slightly altered there: "He took down a book called *Trapping North American Furbearers* by S Stanley Hawbaker" (40).

4. See, for instance, Bell (*Achievement* 31) or Jarrett (14).

5. The *ubi sunt* (Latin for "where are they") motif is originally a lyrical image, commonly used in baroque and romantic poetry, lamenting the vanished past. The attendant *memento mori* (Latin for "remember that you must die") motif is a pictoral or textual image recalling mortality. Equally expressive of a melancholy narrative mood, the *vanitas* (Latin for "vanity" in the sense of "vain effort") motif foregrounds the futility of all human effort in the face of inevitable mortality. All three of these pessimistic motifs are stock elements of the pastoral literature of all ages, designed to qualify the quest for absolute harmony.

6. Ownby's reaction to the conclusion of his annual ritual of cutting a cedar bough for the spray pit confirms his role as a shaman: "And it was done, what soul rose in the ashes forever unknown, out of his hands now. He squatted on one knee in the snow, watching. On his face a suggestion of joy, of anguish—something primitive and half hidden" (158).

7. Another melancholy formula, the *et in Arcadia ego* (Latin for "I, too, am in Arcadia") motif appears first in a baroque painting by Poussin. It is a skull cautioning shepherds in a pastoral landscape to remember their mortality even when in an idyllic place.

8. The idea that Ownby uses the shotgun in the manner of an exorcism is suggested by his intermittent remembrance of having been shot when try-

ing to reclaim his wife (92, 186, 230) and by the ritual aspect of Ownby's firing of the gun: the X-figure shot into the tank, the potshot at the ghostly cat.

9. Most episodes furthering the plot progression are told from the boy's point of view. This explains why he is generally considered the main protagonist even as the title confers this role upon Ownby.

10. That this memory is a key moment is suggested by the circumstances attending its articulation, for they resemble the Eucharist: Ownby offers the boys homemade muscadine wine, and his first flashback occurs after "the old man found the cup of wine in his hand and he regarded it for a moment with mild surprise" (153). Later the sacramental atmosphere is almost made explicit when Ownby, as in a ritual, is "swaying slowly in his rocker holding the cup before him in both hands like a ciborium" (156). Moreover, it is this moment of communion that John Wesley eventually values more than the memory of his mother ("less real than . . . the taste of an old man's wine," 245). The concluding scene repeats the Eucharistic reference in a metaphor of benediction: "The sun broke through the final shelf of clouds and bathed for a moment the dripping trees with blood, tinted the stones a diaphanous wash of color, as if the very air had gone to wine" (246).

11. Pastoral nostalgia does not invalidate the pastoral dream but respects it as an ideal worth pursuing. As Marx writes in reference to *The Great Gatsby,* "The pastoral hope is indicted for its deadly falsity, but the man who clings to it is exonerated" ("Pastoralism" 59).

12. Ownby's character traits also correspond to those of other McCarthy figures who conform to the type of the elder guide. Representatives of this type are the old man with the two hounds that Culla visits in *Outer Dark* (117–29), old Mr. Wade in *Child of God,* old Watson in *Suttree,* the old horseman Luis in *All the Pretty Horses,* the old wolf trapper Don Arnulfo in *The Crossing,* and old Mr. Johnson in *Cities of the Plain.*

13. The moment repeats itself in *All the Pretty Horses* when John Grady's father is "[l]ooking over the country with those sunken eyes as if the world out there had been altered or made suspect by what he'd seen of it elsewhere. As if he might never see it right again. Or worse did see it right at last" (23).

14. The tripartite structure of the novel is also discussed in essays by Arnold and Lang, although in different ways.

15. The distinctions are nowhere near exclusive, because part 1, for instance, contains the subchapters of the harvest (40), the boar hunt (68–69), and the blacksmith (70–74), which are as reflective as anything in part 3 and which are necessary to formulate the traditional pastoral paradigm against which the wilderness turn of parts 2 and 3 defines itself. One of the key moments of narrative melancholia is located in part 1, to wit, the fairground fireworks (65). Similarly, part 3, with its epiphanic thrust, contains long passages emphasizing community interaction (the vigilante episode, 177–86) and reconnecting to the levity of the novel's opening part, with its sympathetic tone of voice and its comic touches (Lester's incarceration and dissection, 193–94). In a sense, of course, part 3 also functions as the plot's denouement by reversing Lester's role from hunting

in part 2 to being himself hunted by Sheriff Fate (a wrecked car is investigated on page 145, a manhunt conducted on page 154) and the vigilantes ("what appeared to be some hunters," 177).

16. McCarthy himself intimated in the interview with Woodward that it was definitely not his intention to seek sympathy for Lester's murders: "Somehow, McCarthy finds compassion for and humor in Ballard, while never asking the reader to forgive his crimes" (31).

17. See essays by Arnold, Bell, Cole, and Ciuba.

18. As an interesting case in point, Lester, in the episode of the fair, becomes a fairground attraction himself, first when he cheats at a game booth (62), then when he displays his marksmanship (64), and later when he carries his prize toy animals around (65).

19. The synchronic diagnosis of the mountain community's affinity to violence is complemented by the diachronic appraisal of the history of local violence as communicated through the intercalary story about vigilantism in the area (165–68) and the account of Lester's ancestors (80–81).

20. Lester's tendency to emulate others becomes apparent earlier when he passes his troubles off on "whiskey or women or both" simply because "[h]e'd often heard men say as much" (53), or when he studies the posters of criminals with assumed identities: "The wanted stared back with surly eyes. Men of many names" (55).

21. Earlier, the Reubel daughter he courts taunts him: "You ain't even a man. You're just a crazy thing" (117).

22. The language of the dream image recurs in a scenic description, signaling that Lester's dream reality and the intra-narrative reality have come to correspond: "[A]s lovely as any day that ever was" finds its analogy in the words "the night being as fine as you could wish" (190). Moreover, the quote illustrates the interaction between wild man Lester and wild nature: Lester "rode" and the leaves "brushed his face," then the leaves "rode over his face" in turn; he "was riding to his death," but the leaves, too, are dying, "already some yellow, their veins like slender bones."

23. The "churchbus" passing Lester suggests that it is indeed Sunday (190).

24. Ditsky argues a similar point, discerning a leveling intent in the "starkness and simplicity" with which the novel portrays its protagonist as on a par with nature. He writes that "more to the point of McCarthy's presentation of his ordinariness, Lester is soon seen urinating, defecating, and masturbating. The atmosphere, particularly within the abandoned house where Lester takes up residence, is one of rot and decay; man is but another particle within a material nature in this novel" (6).

25. The one instant of unadulterated goodness is the spring from which the family taking Rinthy to town stops to drink: "That's fine water, the man said. Fine a water as they is in this country" (69).

26. Satanic connotations mark descriptions of the triune throughout, such as when the leader's "upright shape . . . seemed to be convulsed there for a moment before going from sight like something that had incinerated itself" (168), when the leader answers Culla's question "Where are you bound?" with "I ain't . . . By nothin" (233), and when he answers to Culla's hesitant query regarding his name "I expect they's lots would like to know that"

(175). Because it suggests a split personality, the line "I got Harmon to look after him if *they* do fight" (177–78; emphasis added) seems to link the *nameless* halfwit to the possessed man out of the story of the Gadarene swine whose "name is Legion: for we are many" (Mark 5:9).

27. Arnold thinks it "may in fact (given the circular journeys of the novel) *be* the same glade" ("Naming" 52).

28. Arnold's reading takes its cue from Culla's entry into the glade: "There were three of them and there was a child squatting in the dust and beyond them the tinker's cart with hung pans catching the light like the baleful eyes of some outsized and mute and mindless jury assembled there hurriedly against his coming" (*Outer Dark* 231).

29. Among chances for social reintegration are Rinthy's opportunities to hire out as a "gardener" (98; note the meaning within the pastoral context) or to join a farmer's household (209–11), and Culla's opportunities to trade the boots with the beehiver in order to redeem the theft (80) or to work for the snake hunter (125).

30. Interestingly, Bleikasten mentions that "'Dark House' was the title originally chosen for this novel [*Light in August*], yet even in its absence it is silently at work in the text" (295).

31. Culla is offered redemption several times: The preacher in his dream tells him "Yes, I think perhaps you will be cured" (5), the reverend suggests the possibility of being "saved on the spot" (226), the leader offers him the chance to claim his child (235), the blind man toward the end asks him "Is they anything you need? . . . I'm at the Lord's work" (240). When the blind man suspects that the healer may have been "no true preacher" (241) and that he has meant to relate this suspicion to the man who aborted the healing, he in fact offers redemption as if through a repeal of the patriarchal morality of the novel's pastoral world.

Chapter 2

1. McCarthy's ecocritical angle in *Blood Meridian* is explicitly discussed by Phillips, Pughe, Pilkington, Lilley, Shaviro, and Holloway. The readings not considered here are, for example, those of Jarrett, Daugherty, and Sepich.

2. McCarthy's friendship with the late environmentalist Edward Abbey is common knowledge. A comparison of the quote with the following lines in Abbey's *Desert Solitaire* (1968) confirms the eco-centric leanings of *Blood Meridian:* "The [desert] light is psychedelic, the dry electric air narcotic. To me the desert is stimulating, exciting, exacting; I feel no temptation to sleep or to relax into occult dreams but rather an opposite effect which sharpens and heightens vision, touch, hearing, taste and smell. Each stone, each plant, each grain of sand exists in and for itself with a clarity that is undimmed by any suggestions of a different realm" (155).

3. Elsewhere in the text, the desert in its hostility to human presence is likened to "the face of the planet Anareta" (46), which in Renaissance mythology meant an allegorical planet of death (*see* Daugherty 163).

4. Glanton's hubris (reference the episode in its entirety) actually bears a strange resemblance to Ahab's quarterdeck speech: "Aye, aye! and I'll

chase him round Good Hope, and round the Horn, and round the Norway Maelstrom, and round perdition's flames before I give him up. And this is what ye have shipped for, men! to chase that white whale on both sides of land, and over all sides of earth" (161). In fact, Glanton resembles Ahab in his imperialist ambition more than the judge. If anyone, the judge resembles the diabolic figure of the Parsee Fedallah in *Moby Dick* who, invested with supernatural abilities, presages Ahab's end (491) and is likened to the devil (324).

5. Tobin remarks, "Glanton I always knew was mad" (127) and "he seemed to have had his wits stole" (133). At Jesús María, "Glanton in his drunkenness was taken with a kind of fit and he lurched crazed and disheveled into the little courtyard and began to open fire with his pistols. In the afternoon he lay bound to his bed like a madman" (191).

6. In this context, McCarthy's prolix choice of register seems to pose something of a problem. One could argue that if you were entirely determined to strip your fictional universe of all that is human—to "wipe your fingerprints off the landscape"—you simply would not choose such arcane vocabulary. You'd keep language as plain and monosyllabic, as organic, indeed as "optically democratic" as possible. That is, unless words as linguistic facts are considered, in turn, the equal of natural facts (not in a transcendentalist but an ecosophical sense), and either as simple or as complex as organic can be.

7. John Sepich excerpted from *Blood Meridian* a lengthy concordance labeled "Hallucinatory Void" (142–45).

8. Abbey mentions a very similar list, posted in an outhouse at Arches National Monument, and if this is indeed an intertextual moment inspiring McCarthy's image, then the desert outhouse is in turn a locus of a precarious existential truce between nature and man: "Attention: Watch out for rattlesnakes, coral snakes, whip snakes, vinegaroons, centipedes, millipedes, ticks, mites, black widows, cone-nosed kissing bugs, solpugids, tarantulas, horned toads, Gila monsters, red ants, fire ants, Jerusalem crickets, cinch bugs and Giant Hairy Desert Scorpions before being seated" (35).

9. The kid's indifference is pinpointed by the judge's rejoinder to the kid's evasive speculation as to the purpose of his and other inngoers' presence in the saloon: "That's so, said the judge. They do not have to have a reason. But order is not set aside because of their indifference" (328).

10. The analogy is corroborated by the letters tattooed into Toadvine's forehead just like the *shem* placed on the Golem's forehead to waken him to life: "His head was strangely narrow and his hair was plastered up with mud in a bizarre and primitive coiffure. On his forehead were burned the letters H T and lower and almost between the eyes the letter F" (11).

11. Quoted from the instructions (30) enclosed in the Rider Tarot Deck by U.S. Game Systems, and originally excerpted from *The Key to the Tarot* by Arthur Edward White.

12. As the kid tries to take his pleasure against better knowledge, ignoring the judge's warning "Drink up. This night thy soul may be required of thee" (327), he succumbs to the false equanimity of the rich man of Christ's parable who tells himself "take thine ease, eat, drink, and be merry," and

to whom God replies, "Thou fool, this night thy soul shall be required of thee" (Luke 12:19–20).

13. Kristeva's words are strangely paraphrased in the description of the kid's nightmare of the coldforger who is "an exile . . . hammering . . . all through the night of his becoming . . . and the night does not end" (310).

14. The one other time that the kid is referred to as "child" is during the prison scene when he is plagued by dreams of the judge, in whose eyes "this child just sixteen years on earth could read whole bodies of decisions not accountable to the course of men and he saw his own name which nowhere else could he have ciphered out at all logged into the records as a thing already accomplished" (310). Read allegorically, the passage describes him as a type whose biography is preordained by the typological role model of the failed picaro.

15. Interestingly, the halfwit James Robert Bell, grouped with the novel's infants because the text once calls him "this child" (258), is similarly described as having "dark larval eyes" (282).

16. The intertextuality with Dante is suggested by the use of the rare word "stobs" in both texts, and in the description of the selfsame landscape as a "terra damnata" (*Meridian* 61) and a "purgatorial waste" (*Meridian* 63).

17. The association of "see the child" with the "ecce homo" motif points to the humanist tradition that the novel abandons and also to the designation of the kid as "the child." In fact, this substitution might be seen as part of the larger paradigm shift from a traditional pastoral to a radical wilderness view: "The kid" is a less culturally charged, arguably more "organic" (in its use for both human and animal offspring), deracinated (in that it does not imply parentage and origin as much as "child" does) version of the same semantic concept. Even inasmuch as both terms point to cultural traditions, "child" is associated with civilization (Childe Roland), while "kid" conjures the Wild West (Billy the Kid).

18. Interestingly, Benjamin mentions a similar scene, Herod's infanticide, as typical for baroque drama, showing "the seventeenth century sovereign, the paragon of creation, erupting into rage like a volcano and annihilating himself along with the entire court around him. Paintings reveled in the image of how he, holding two infants in his hands in order to smash them, succumbs to madness" (*Trauerspiel* 52). The scene also recalls the lament of Israel in exile: "O daughter of Babylon, who art to be destroyed; happy shall he be, that rewardeth thee as thou hast served us. Happy shall he be, that taketh and dasheth thy little ones against the stones" (Ps. 137:8–9).

19. For a history of the aphorism see Panofsky's essay "Et in Arcadio Ego," reprinted, among other places, in Eleanor T. Lincoln, ed., *Pastoral and Romance,* Englewood Cliffs, N.J.: Prentice Hall, 1969, 25–46.

20. The line that Tonio Kröger recalls as he nostalgically watches an almost maniacal dance scene states inversely: "Ich möchte schlafen, aber du musst tanzen," (I want to sleep, but you must dance). It is in turn borrowed from Theodor Storm's poem "Hyazinthen," also describing an interminable dance (see Sepich 170–71). The subchapter heading in *Blood Meridian* translates as "You must sleep, but I must dance," suggesting that Death is speaking to the kid and euphemizing his imminent death as a sleep.

21. The image of Death as a horseman recalls the tarot card "Death," which in the Rider deck depicts a mounted skeleton riding down people of all social strata. The tarot image reconnects to the typological tradition of the four apocalyptic horsemen of Revelations, one of whom is Death.

22. The ecocritical context of this statement is established by the circumstance that it responds to the query as to "whether there were on Mars or other planets in the void men or creatures like them" (245). The buffalo hunter, upon conclusion of his tale of the extinction of the buffalo, asks the same question: "I wonder if there's other worlds like this" (317). The text offers no answer (the subchapter ends with the question), and so the answer given earlier by the judge applies.

Chapter 3

1. Toward the end, the wolves become emblematic of Billy's melancholia. In a dream that contains his moribund brother as well, the wolves come up to him and "when the last of them had come forward they stood in a crescent before him and their eyes were like footlights to the ordinate world" (*Crossing* 295).

2. An intertextual reference to the equally anachronistic *Don Quixote,* the knight of the sad countenance, is implied in Billy's realization that "riding so armed [with bow and arrow] in his blackened rags atop the bony horse he must cut a sad or foolish figure" (*Crossing* 132).

3. In his rhetoric and arrogance, the Native American oddly resembles the triune's leader in *Outer Dark.*

4. The concluding lines reconnect to Hemingway's title *The Sun Also Rises* and moreover to the source that Hemingway quotes in that novel's epigraph, which is Ecclesiastes 1:4–6: "One generation passeth away, and another generation cometh: but the earth abideth for ever. The sun also ariseth, and the sun goeth down, and hasteth to the place where he arose." The ending of *The Crossing* groups the novel openly with the typology of *vanitas* allegoresis. It also calls to mind the above-quoted passage in *Child of God* (170), in which Lester Ballard squats down in similar posture and begins to cry. If nothing else, McCarthy uses the same paradigmatic scene to show the progressing aesthetic development of his protagonists.

5. *Cities of the Plain* "has existed for more than 10 years as a screenplay" (Woodward 40) now in the possession of the McCarthy Collection of the Texas State University–San Marcos. See Arnold's article "First Thoughts" for a comparison of the screenplay with the novel.

6. The proverbial sinfulness of the cities of the plain, which are Sodom and Gomorrah ("God destroyed the cities of the plain," Gen. 20:29), is discussed by Billy and the Mormon in *The Crossing.* Billy asks, "You think maybe the people that lived there had done something bad?" and the Mormon answers, "I thought it possible, yes. As in the cities of the plain" (142). The urban environment of *Cities of the Plain* is thereby identified as evil, quite in tune with any pastoral tenets, conventional or ecosophical.

7. As argued earlier, the picaresque genre as such is allegorical by nature. *Huckleberry Finn,* for one, becomes a psychosocial sketch of the antebellum South if one reads the novel allegorically.

8. See the Woodward article for McCarthy's reservations regarding the success of *All the Pretty Horses.*

9. "Melancholy gaze" is to be understood here as a cognitive automatism that causes the observer to associate mortality or transience with any object that he or she beholds.

10. The posthumous perspective of storytelling is dramatized in John Grady's dream in which he asks Blevins's ghost "what it was like to be dead and Blevins said it was like nothing at all and he believed him" (*Horses* 225).

11. The argument owes its gist to "The Storyteller," differentiating "between him who records history, the historian, and him who narrates it, the chronicler" (Benjamin, *Illuminationen* 397).

12. The Spanish words translate into "face and reverse" (of the coin).

13. Vega translates into "(fertile) flatland" and Víbora into "viper," so that the place names become allegorical of the world's oscillation between life and death. That this allegorical magic of names is intended is confirmed by the use of these names in *Outer Dark,* in which Rinthy travels "in the cold starlight, under vega and the waterserpent" (211), in limbo between life and death, as the use of the constellations suggests.

14. The idea that darkness constitutes the essence of the world is paralleled in the oxherd's observation that "the ox was an animal close to God as all the world knew and that perhaps the silence and the rumination of the ox was something like the shadow of a greater silence, a deeper thought" (*Crossing* 235–36).

15. The Spanish words translate into "I am the commander of the mares . . . me and only me."

16. Poland relies for his concept of the eco-hero on Joseph Campbell's definition of the mythological hero in *The Hero with a Thousand Faces* (1949).

17. Poland actually rephrases the tenor of relevant essays in Aldo Leopold's *A Sand County Almanac* (1949).

18. An example of such literature would again be *Desert Solitaire,* in which Abbey proposes that "the wilderness should be preserved for political reasons. We may need it someday not only as a refuge from excessive industrialism but also as a refuge from authoritarian government, from political oppression" (149).

19. Love rephrases the definition given by Roderick Nash in *Wilderness and the American Mind.*

20. The contrast between John Grady's pastoral idealism and his father's resignation may explain why the protagonist is never referred to by his patronym but is instead called John Grady throughout the Trilogy, after his maternal line of ancestors, "the wild Grady boys" (301).

21. The image prefigures the coming years of drought mentioned in *Cities of the Plain* (264). It also calls to mind Albert Bierstadt's painting "The Last of the Buffalo," and thus the extermination of the buffalo narrated in *Blood Meridian* (316–17), as if to trace a karmic aspect in the failure of cattle ranching in West Texas.

22. In *All the Pretty Horses,* the aggressively exploitative attitude toward nature is exemplified by the "oilfield scouts' cars parked along the street that

looked like they'd been in a warzone" (11), cars that help implement land management for maximum efficiency.

Conclusion

1. Bakhtin gives "the name *chronotope* (literally, 'time space') to the intrinsic connectedness of temporal and spatial relationships that are artistically expressed in literature. [. . .] In the literary artistic chronotope, spatial and temporal indicators are fused into one carefully thought-out, concrete whole" (*Dialogic Imagination* 84).

Works Cited

McCarthy Editions Cited

McCarthy, Cormac. *Blood Meridian, or the Evening Redness in the* West. New York: Vintage, 1992.

———. *Suttree*. New York: Vintage, 1992.

———. *All the Pretty Horses*. New York: Vintage, 1993.

———. *Child of God*. New York: Vintage, 1993.

———. *Outer Dark*. New York: Vintage, 1993.

———. *The Orchard Keeper.* New York: Vintage, 1993.

———. *The Crossing.* New York: Vintage, 1995.

———. *Cities of the Plain*. New York: Vintage, 1999.

Secondary Works

Note: All translations of Benjamin and other German sources are my own.

Abbey, Edward. *Desert Solitaire. A Season in the Wilderness*. New York: Ballantine, 1971.

Aldridge, John W. "Cormac McCarthy's Bizarre Genius." *Atlantic Monthly*, August, 1994.

Arnold, Edwin T. "The Last of the Trilogy: First Thoughts on *Cities of the Plain*." In *Perspectives on Cormac McCarthy*. rev. ed. Ed. Edwin T. Arnold and Dianne C. Luce. Jackson: University Press of Mississippi, 1999.

———. "Naming, Knowing and Nothingness: McCarthy's Moral Parables." In *Perspectives on Cormac McCarthy*. rev. ed. Edited by Edwin T. Arnold and Dianne C. Luce. Jackson: University Press of Mississippi, 1999.

Bakhtin, Mikhail M. *The Dialogic Imagination*. Austin: The University of Texas Press, 1981.

———. *Rabelais and His World*. Bloomington: Indiana University Press, 1984.

Bartlett, Andrew. "From Voyeurism to Archaeology: Cormac McCarthy's *Child of God*." *Southern Literary Journal* 24, no. 4 (Fall 1992): 3–15.

Bell, Vereen M. *The Achievement of Cormac McCarthy*. Baton Rouge: Louisiana State University Press, 1988.

———. "The Ambiguous Nihilism of Cormac McCarthy." *Southern Literary Journal* 15, no. 2 (Spring 1983): 31–41.

Benjamin, Walter. *Illuminationen*. Frankfurt: Suhrkamp, 1977.

———. *Ursprung des deutschen Trauerspiels*. Frankfurt: Suhrkamp, 1978.

Blanchot, Maurice. "The Two Versions of the Imaginary." In *The Space of Literature*. Lincoln: University of Nebraska Press, 1989.

Bleikasten, André. *The Ink of Melancholy*. Bloomington: Indiana University Press, 1990.

Boothby, Richard. *Death and Desire. Psychoanalytic Theory in Lacan's Return to Freud*. New York: Routledge, 1991.

Buell, Lawrence. "American Pastoral Ideology Reappraised." *American Literary History* 1, no. 1 (Spring 1989): 1–29.

Charyn, James. "Doomed Huck." *New York Times Book Review*, February 18, 1979.

Ciuba, Gary M. "McCarthy's Enfant Terrible: Mimetic Desire and Sacred Violence in *Child of God*." In *Sacred Violence. A Reader's Companion to Cormac McCarthy*. Edited by Wade Hall and Rick Wallach. El Paso: Texas Western Press, 1995.

Daugherty, Leo. "Gravers False and True: *Blood Meridian* as Gnostic Tragedy." In *Perspectives on Cormac McCarthy*. rev. ed. Ed. Edwin T. Arnold and Dianne C. Luce. Jackson: University Press of Mississippi, 1999.

Davenport, Guy. "Appalachian Gothic." *New York Times Book Review*, September 29, 1968.

De Man, Paul. "The Rhetoric of Temporality." In *Critical Theory Since 1965*. Edited by Hazard Adams and Leroy Searle. Tallahassee: Florida State University Press, 1986.

Ditsky, John. "Further Into Darkness: The Novels of Cormac McCarthy." *Hollins Critic* 18, no. 2 (April, 1981): 1–11.

Donoghue, Denis. "Dream Work." *New York Review of Books*, June 24, 1993.

Donne, John. "Meditation XVII." In *The Complete Poetry and Selected Prose of John Donne*. Edited by Charles M. Coffin. New York: Random House, 1952.

Eliot, T. S. "The Waste Land." In *The Norton Anthology of Modern Poetry*. 2nd ed. Edited by Richard Ellman and Robert O'Clair. New York: Norton, 1988.

Faulkner, William. *Light in August*. New York: Vintage, 1990.

———. *The Sound and the Fury*. New York: Vintage, 1987.

Fletcher, Angus. *Allegory. The Theory of a Symbolic Mode*. Ithaca: Cornell University Press, 1964.

Grammer, John M. "A Thing Against Which Time Will Not Prevail: Pastoral and History in Cormac McCarthy's South." In *Perspectives on Cormac McCarthy*. rev. ed. Edited by Edwin T. Arnold and Dianne C. Luce. Jackson: University Press of Mississippi, 1999.

Hass, Robert. "Travels With A She-Wolf." *New York Times Book Review*, June 12, 1994.

Hillman, James. "Senex and Puer: An Aspect of the Historical and Psychological Present." In *Puer Papers*. Edited by James Hillman, et al. Irving: Spring Publications, 1979.

Holloway, David. "Modernism, Nature, and Utopia: Another Look at 'Optical Democracy' in Cormac McCarthy's Western Quartet." *Southern Quarterly* 38, no. 3 (Spring 2000): 186–205.

James, William. *The Varieties of Religious Experience*. Harmondsworth, England: Penguin, 1982.

Jarrett, Robert L. *Cormac McCarthy*. New York: Twayne, 1997.

Kerr, Elisabeth M. *William Faulkner's Gothic Domain*. Port Washington, N.Y.: Kennikat Press, 1979.

Kreml, Nancy. "Stylistic Variations and Cognitive Constraints in *All the Pretty Horses*." In *Sacred Violence. A Reader's Companion to Cormac McCarthy*. Edited by Wade Hall and Rick Wallach. El Paso: Texas Western Press, 1995.

Kristeva, Julia. *Black Sun. Depression and Melancholia*. New York: Columbia University Press, 1989.

———. *Powers of Horror. An Essay on Abjection*. New York: Columbia University Press, 1982.

Kroeber, Karl. *Ecological Literary Criticism. Romantic Imagining and the Biology of Mind*. New York: Columbia University Press, 1994.

Lacan, Jacques. *Ecrits. A Selection*. New York: Norton, 1977.

Lang, John. "Lester Ballard: McCarthy's Challenge to the Reader's Compassion." In *Sacred Violence. A Reader's Companion to Cormac McCarthy*. Edited by Wade Hall and Rick Wallach. El Paso: Texas Western Press, 1995.

Leiter, Robert. "Child of God." *Commonweal*, March 29, 1974.

Lilley, James. "Representing Cormac McCarthy's 'Desert Absolute': Edward Weston, Ansel Adams, and the Dynamics of Vision." In *Proceedings of the Second Annual International Conference on the Emerging Literature of the Southwest*. El Paso: University of Texas, 1996.

Longley, John Lewis, Jr. "Suttree and the Metaphysics of Death." *Southern Literary Journal* 17, no. 2 (Spring 1985): 79–90.

Love, Glen A. "*Et in Arcadia Ego:* Pastoral Theory Meets Ecocriticism." *Western American Literature* 27, no. 3 (Fall 1992): 195–207.

Luce, Dianne C. "The Voice of the Orchard: An Eco-critical Reading of *The Orchard Keeper.*" Unpublished typescript for the Second European Conference on Cormac McCarthy, Manchester, England, 2000.

Madsen, Deborah L. *Allegory in America. From Puritanism to Postmodernism.* London: Macmillan, 1996.

Manes, Christopher. "Nature and Silence." In *The Ecocriticism Reader. Landmarks in Literary Ecology.* Edited by Cheryll Glotfelty and Harold Fromm. Athens: University of Georgia Press, 1996.

Marx, Leo. *The Machine in the Garden. Technology and the Pastoral Ideal in America.* New York: Oxford University Press, 1964.

———. "Pastoralism in America." *Ideology and Classic American Literature.* Edited by Sacvan Bercovitch and Myra Jehlen. Cambridge: Cambridge University Press, 1987.

Meeker, Joseph W. *The Comedy of Survival. Literary Ecology and a Play Ethic.* 3rd ed. Tucson: University of Arizona Press, 1997.

Melville, Herman. *Moby Dick, or The Whale.* New York: Modern Library, 1950.

Mills, Jerry Leath. "Cormac McCarthy (1933–)." In *Contemporary Fiction Writers of the South.* Edited by Joseph M. Flora and Robert Bain. Westport, Conn.: Greenwood, 1993.

Morrison, Gail M. "*All the Pretty Horses:* John Grady Cole's Expulsion from Paradise." In *Perspectives on Cormac McCarthy.* rev. ed. Edited by Edwin T. Arnold and Dianne C. Luce. Jackson: University Press of Mississippi, 1999.

Nash, Roderick. *Wilderness and the American Mind.* 3rd ed. New Haven: Yale University Press, 1982.

Neihardt, John G. *Black Elk Speaks.* New York: Pocket Books, 1972.

Owens, Craig. "The Allegorical Impulse: Toward a Theory of Postmodernism." In *Art After Modernism. Rethinking Representation.* Edited by Brian Wallis. New York: New Museum of Contemporary Art, 1984.

Phillips, Dana. "History and the Ugly Facts of Cormac McCarthy's *Blood Meridian.*" *American Literature* 68, no. 2 (June, 1996): 433–60.

———. "Is Nature Necessary?" In *The Ecocriticism Reader. Landmarks in Literary Ecology.* Edited by Cheryll Glotfelty and Harold Fromm. Athens: University of Georgia Press, 1996.

Pilkington, Tom. "Fate and Free Will on the American Frontier: Cormac McCarthy's Western Fiction." *Western American Fiction* 27, no. 4 (Winter 1993): 311–22.

Poland, Tim. "'A Relative to All That Is': The Eco-Hero in Western American Literature." *Western American Literature* 26, no. 3 (Fall 1991): 195–208.

Prescott, Orville. "Still Another Disciple of William Faulkner." *New York Times,* May 12, 1965.

Pughe, Thomas. "Revision and Vision: Cormac McCarthy's *Blood Meridian.*" *Revue Française d'Etudes Américaines* 17, no. 62 (November, 1994): 371–82.

Ragan, David Paul. "Values and Structure in *The Orchard Keeper.*" In *Perspectives on Cormac McCarthy.* rev. ed. Edited by Edwin T. Arnold and Dianne C. Luce. Jackson: University Press of Mississippi, 1999.

Schafer, William J. "Cormac McCarthy: The Hard Wages of Original Sin." *Appalachian Journal* 4 (Winter 1977): 105–19.

Schleifer, Ronald. "Walter Benjamin and the Crisis of Representation: Multiplicity, Meaning, and Athematic Death." *Death and Representation.* Edited by Sarah W. Goodwin and Elisabeth Bronfen. Baltimore: Johns Hopkins University Press, 1993.

Schopen, Bernard A. "'They Rode On': *Blood Meridian* and the Art of Narrative." *Western American Literature* 30, no. 2 (Summer 1995): 179–94.

Sepich, John Emil. *Notes on Blood Meridian.* Louisville: Bellarmine College Press, 1993.

Shaviro, Steven. "'The Very Life of Darkness:' A Reading of *Blood Meridian.*" *Perspectives on Cormac McCarthy.* rev. ed. Edited by Edwin T. Arnold and Dianne C. Luce. Jackson: University Press of Mississippi, 1999.

Shelton, Frank W. "Suttree and Suicide." *Southern Quarterly* 29, no. 1 (Fall 1990): 71–83.

Simpson, Lewis P. *The Dispossessed Garden. Pastoral and History in Southern Literature.* Athens: University of Georgia Press, 1975.

Sullivan, Walter. "Worlds Past and Future: A Christian and Several from the South." *Sewanee Review* 73, no. 4 (Fall 1965): 719–26.

———. "'Where Have All The Flowers Gone?' Part II: The Novel in the Gnostic Twilight." *Sewanee Review* 78, no. 4 (Fall 1970): 654–64.

———. "Model Citizens and Marginal Cases: Heroes of the Day." *Sewanee Review* 87, no. 2 (Spring 1979): 337–43.

Trachtenberg, Stanley. "Black Humor, Pale Fiction." *Yale Review* 55, no. 1 (Fall 1965): 144–49.

Trotignon, Beatrice. "The Inscription of an Impersonal Lyricism." Unpublished typescript for the Second European Conference on Cormac McCarthy, Manchester, England, 2000.

———. "The Workings of 'and' in *Child of God:* 'a Succession of Strobic Moments'." Unpublished typescript for the Annual International Conference on Cormac McCarthy, El Paso, Texas, 1999.

Wallace, Garry. "Meeting McCarthy." *Southern Quarterly* 30, no. 4 (Summer 1992): 134–42.

Whitman, Walt. *Poetry and Prose.* New York: Library of America, 1982.

Winchell, Mark Royden. "Inner Dark, or The Place of Cormac McCarthy." *Southern Review* 26 (April, 1990): 293–309.

Woodward, Richard B. "Cormac McCarthy's Venomous Fiction." *New York Times Magazine.* April 19, 1992.

Young, Thomas D., Jr. "The Imprisonment of Sensibility: *Suttree.*" *Perspectives on Cormac McCarthy.* rev. ed. Edited by Edwin T. Arnold and Dianne C. Luce. Jackson: University Press of Mississippi, 1999.

Index

ISBN 1-58544-341-7